OUT OF THE INTERIOR

OTHER BOOKS BY HAROLD RHENISCH

Six Poets of British Columbia (Sono Nis Press, 1980)

Winter (Sono Nis Press, 1981)

Eleusis (Sono Nis Press, 1986)

A Delicate Fire (Sono Nis Press, 1989)

Dancing with My Daughter (Sono Nis Press, 1993)

OUT OF THE INTERIOR

The Lost Country

by

Harold Rhenisch

OUT OF THE INTERIOR
Copyright © 1993 Harold Rhenisch

CACANADADADA PRESS LTD.
3350 West 21st Avenue
Vancouver, B.C. Canada
V6S 1G7

Set in Baskerville 10½ pt on 13½
Typesetting: The Typeworks, Vancouver, B.C.
Printing: Hignell Printing, Winnipeg, Manitoba
Cover Design: Cecilia Jang
Cover Art: Alvin Jang

The publisher wishes to thank the Canada Council and the British Columbia Cultural Services Branch for their generous financial assistance.

CANADIAN CATALOGUING IN PUBLICATION DATA

Rhenisch, Harold, 1958–
   Out of the interior

   ISBN 0-921870-23-X
   I. Title.
PS8585.H5408 1993   C813'.54   C93-091030-3
PR9199.3.R5208 1993

DEDICATION

This book is for Hans Rhenisch

Acknowledgements

A selection from the early part of this manuscript appeared in *Event*.

CONTENTS

Prologue

ADRIFT IN THE stone troughs of the mountains of the Interior, two hundred miles inland from the Pacific and the world, the possibility, in this lost colonial island, of approaching a sense of country and culture through History exists only in the gathering of a few scraps and ruins. This is an abandoned country, and it is being re-colonized. What is being colonized, or exploited, today, is not the earth that was colonized in the past, but the culture that grew out of that approach, the images of the land in which I first walked, surrounded by birds and sun and wind. The real Okanagan, as it has evolved out of its own history and its own forms, still, however, exists: Jake van Westen in Naramata, replanting his orchard with vision and, what is rare among orchardists today, a sense of future, of continuation in time; Hugh Dendy in East Kelowna, bitterly watching from his cherry orchard on the sand hills above Mission Creek the orchard culture of East Kelowna wither under suburban pressure; Bill Embrey in Vancouver, who left for university twenty years ago and who can only visit now as a foreigner, forever an exile, with no past, only memories, and no possibility of return. The vision is there, the stunted forms are there, the articulation and intelligence are there.

My own sense of history in the Okanagan and my perceptual sense of its land forms are bound intimately with the dreams and visions that my father imported from Europe. Although he made every effort to integrate culturally, and in many ways did so successfully, the integration was never complete. As a result, my Canada is not the Canada of my friends, who lived on orchards just a few hundred yards down the road, but a unique world, part Okanagan, part Germany, and part transcendent vision. This estrangement has at times seemed a curse, but it has enabled me to see clearly the half-formed and interrupted growth of this country and the failure of language: our inability to speak of our own history as it actually determines the boundaries of our lives, and the possibilities within it for true independence and liberation.

For years it has disturbed me that my mother does not show up as large in these pages as my father. I used to dismiss this lack by accepting that she has chosen, or has been given, the path of invisibility in this world, but that is a failure of perception: she is present in every page here, just as my father is, but where my father's presence is loud, strong, sometimes intrusive, and always verbal and active, my mother's is subtle and withdrawn; she exists in the landscape, the actual, physical perception and articulation of sun and air and leaf and soil and flower, that world my father skittered over, was sustained by, yet could hardly touch, could only see—frustrated—through a veil. It is through her that the world comes clear, and lives.

This book is obviously cathartic, but cathartic in the specific sense of Greek tragedy, of paying for the sins of our ancestors, of humankind trapped by a relentless fate yet made human by that cage. Ironically, now that I have finished this book as a tragedy, its story is becoming a comedy: after sixteen years of exile, my father has bought an orchard in Oliver and is right now walking down his heavily-blossomed rows, lifted out of himself, at the centre of the world, alive, and my mother, too, is out of the concrete city again, away from the sulfurous air of the oil refinery at Port Moody, and again inside her perceptions. Even so, it may well be that these choices can be made by men and women of my parents' generation, while for us, their heirs, exiled by land-speculation and banished by the barriers of a foreign education, the choice of moving into direct perception of the physical world through the simple purchase of land is impossible. Whether we ever find a way to re-enter the land or not, right now it is only through words and a re-shaping of perception that we can enter our country and ensure its existence in the world. Although the forces arrayed against us, not the least of which are the very notions of property, so central to my parents' generation, are strong, our task, as has been the task of every generation before us, is to speak into the void and to give it form—it is to return the world to life.

April 22, 1992
Keremeos, B.C.

I
My Father's Hands

A World of Water

MY FATHER HAD small hands. They were the thin, clumsy hands of his mind. Some days they were hot and red, the nails ground down into small, delicate hooves. Some days they were white and cold and afraid. Through those hands he saw the world. When his eyes settled on an apple, a Macintosh, white with wax and yeast, that whole day before him drained immediately down out of the air and through his nerves into his hands, and they tried to grab it. In this way he attempted to make some sense of this world of things.

In spring, with the light like saffron in the air, a thin wind fusing the sage pollen with the heat off the shale, he would walk out into the bright fields of dandelions under the trees. In the week before the apples blossomed, storms that had come two hundred miles over the mountains from the sea broke over the ridges and filled the valley with a liquid light, surging over him, there at the bottom of the sky, in slow, cool currents. When the trees at last flared into bloom, he would sit in the cool basement, poring over spray charts, calibration rates, pounds per acre, Guthion 50% WP, Malathion, Thiodan. Around him even the house would tremble as she smelled the change on the wind, and she would rise to it, unsteady on her legs. Each year for a few weeks she would come to life, at blossom time, when the air would smell of the water pouring like a river up through the roots and then out through all the new leaves of the trees, then she would collapse again, like a dry insect casing, into the gravel.

My father's hands always looked helpless, feverish, burning away the cold of the Uncle Ben's Malt Liquor—a green beer with a green plaid label: "A maverick too!" he'd say, looking up, bloodshot. His eyes would be small then, and such an ozone-blue they seemed to be chips of lapis lazuli, dug out of a damp, muddy barrow. They gave no appearance of usefulness. They did not seem eyes a man could see with, or through which an entire day could flood, filling his body with a late spring afternoon of pink-edged apple-blossoms, and icy rain sinking off the snow-choked peaks of the valley wall. They gave only one impression: of terror, of a god living there who did not need them to confront the world, but who was saddled with them and was utterly terrified of what he saw. My father's eyes were an extension of his body, of the energy in his chest with which he met the world, hardly needing to draw a breath, and, most of all, a reaching forth of his hands.

The Days of Dust

THOSE WERE the years of wonders, years of uprooted apricots, old tires soaked in diesel oil and thrown under the shattered piles of trees to start them into fire, years of flame, a sun so thin it filled the entire sky, right down to the surface of the soil. Through the columns of black diesel smoke that tore through the mounds of trees, choking with dust and ash and steam from the wet wood, it was a sun on fire. Those were the years the oxygen was burning out of the air. Where before there had been trees and grass and quiet, now there was dust and the desert stars, like welding arcs in the hull of a ship being built for war.

On one of those long, dusty days, with a wind passing at great speed behind the thin light, a young eagle landed on the ripped-up sod, but could not climb again. Otto and my father brought it in at coffee-time, in its stone feathers. All day it ate thin strips of bacon, smashing down at them viciously with its hooked, yellow beak. At dusk, as the fires raged into the thin sky, throwing long shadows over the fields, they tossed it in the trunk of the Biscayne and drove it up to Barcelo Canyon. There, in the sage and rabbitbush below the cliffs, they set it loose. It huddled on the ground as the first stars burned through the air and the wind began to pour out of the stone.

Those were the years of Vietnam, when the US fighters often swept over the border at the bottom of the valley. While our fighters raced to intercept them, leaving white streams and loops of vapour in the gritty cloudless air, we'd stand for hours on the edge of the gravel bank, staring up at them, the dog at our sides, thrusting his muzzle up at the sun and crooning.

Beethoven's Sixth

You know, I'd like to go back there, to walk down the driveway to my first land, an army-surplus duffle-bag thrown over my shoulder. While my father sat out on the porch in the sage-wind and the sprinkler wind of evening, the light pouring out of the air like water out of an open pipe, the whole house booming so loudly with that scratched-up record of Beethoven's *Pastorale* that you could not stand inside, I'd like to walk up the steps to where he sat on the sun-rotted fibreglass of his deck-chair beating out the rhythm with his stubby brown beer bottle, conducting us—"See! Can't you hear the thunder? IIa!"—and slap him out of it, for I have that record now and it is so scratched, and, like a photograph, faded, its tone flat, half-erased by use and time, that it carries little of those years, and I am not walking back down a driveway but only sitting here at my window late at night as my wife and daughters sleep and the wind tears through my fingers and my mouth and my bones and my eyes, listening to music in my head.

Time-Waves

IN THOSE DAYS of old British Columbia, cut off from the world, cut off by horizons of stone and cottonwoods, mountain goats like spills of old lead paint rising and falling through colour like whitecaps on the sea, my father was out with his insect screen, tapping on the tree branches with a sawed-off broom handle. On a white piece of cotton torn out of a sheet and stretched over a foot-square wooden frame, he caught the insects that jarred off the branches: thrips, pamplamona, aphids, mites, spiders; and then knelt down in the grass to count them—to time his sprays. All around him the meadowlarks hollered through the air from power poles or the top, soft tips of trees, anywhere high and thin and alone and wooden, to claim their space, yellow-breasted echoings across time.

Herb Tea

My MOTHER LIVED inside, behind the calcium-stained glass of the windows, struggling to become invisible, just as her mother, in her last years, desperately tried to remember the herbs her own mother in turn had collected from the fields around Breslau—but it was too much to recall. Short, fat, and arthritic, each fall my grandmother would collect rosehips and alfalfa and nettles, for the same reason her mother picked them to try to deaden the stone and coal of a great European industrial city—to bring the fields of her childhood close—my grandmother would sit over a cup of tea in the evenings and pour those hot yellow cups of light, with their scents of hay and rain, down her throat, with hardly a flinch. They would seep down through all her veins until they collected in her bones. And her bones would glow.

In our family generations on generations of women have lived their cramped lives in this way, all the way back to the first Marsel, young German girlfriend of a soldier of Napoleon's army, who, when the French withdrew, decided to stay, so far from home, for love. And all the way back before that, generation upon generation of cramped women trying to remember and even to re-create, to cup between the hands and so to transfer, the light.

A Solar Collector

WORK DID not make my father free, but it did almost oblit-
erate the living earth: Rosy Apple Aphid, Ambrosia Beetle,
European Red Mite, Bruce Spanworm, Leafroller, Budmoth,
Campylomma, Green Fruitworm, Thrips, Codling Moth,
Leafhopper, Wooly Aphid, Green Apple Aphid, Rust Mite,
McDaniel Mite, Two-spotted Spider Mite, spiders, ants that
climbed the trees to milk the aphids like cattle for their nectar;
all delicate, pin-heads scampering over the white cloth, dazed
by the light it collects.

Once my father had counted his catch he would move a few
rows down the orchard, and tap another branch lightly, "thap
thap." The sound would echo dully through the trees, row on
row on row through the orchard, like waves slowly dulling as
they pushed their way onto shore, under the liquid sun.

The Last Working Hardy
Sprayer in British Columbia

From time to time you can still see these old, rusty hulks, their tires grey and crumbling, behind dry-rotted prop-piles in the waste-ground of orchards, the long vines and small dust-flowers of wild clematis tangled through their fans—relics from the days of death just after the War. Before their arrival the orchards were doused by hand-held hoses—the sprays were piped through the water system: lime-sulphur, arsenic of lead, and nicotine. On many of the old orchards it is now hard to get a tree to flourish since the lead arsenic has so tightly bound with the alkali in the soil that the nutrients cannot be picked up by the roots. The trees grow stunted, as if planted on a marsh. The Hardy sprayer is such a sprayer, but with a clumsy gasoline-powered blower added at the back for automatic application of the new chemicals of the War: Guthion, for one—developed as a nerve gas, for combat. It has a distinct, harsh, lung-tightening smell. If you walk into an orchard anywhere on this continent, more than any wine of fruit or grass or rain it will be Guthion you smell. Its residue stays for days in the skin. The most strongly-held belief of farmers is that the skin is a form of leather, impervious to all compounds, a magical bone-tight clothing protecting us from the world.

In Kelowna once, in the summer of rain, when the grass never dried out underfoot and great black scabs of fungus spread across the skins of the apples in a slow marking of time,

I tasted Guthion. In the shelter of a few scraggly young cotton-woods that had sprung up through the wild roses covering the sweating aluminum water main, I opened a bag of Guthion and drank it as a gust of wind tore around the side of the sap-lings and through a small crack where the rubber and paper canister mask didn't fit tightly to my chin. There in the tall wet grass and the dandelions soft-stemmed from all the rain I lay for ten minutes, hardly able to breathe, nothing over me but a shattered blue and black sky that looked thinner than ever, and floating away.

Guthion was used against our main prey—codling moth. These small, dusty-grey moths lay their eggs on the skin of ap-ples and pears. When the eggs hatch, the larvae, white, black-headed worms, burrow through the fruit and eat the seeds, then burrow out again, drop down, and pupate, a foot down in the soil, only to come out again in a few weeks as new moths. All the time the face of the fruit is covered with a dry brown sawdust. As the years went by we saw more and more codlers as my father cut back farther and farther on the dosage of his sprays, as he grew more and more sick.

Agent Orange

THOSE WERE the days of the War in Vietnam, and the *Good Fruit Grower* magazine, from Yakima, Washington, grew fat with chemical ads, all laid out in terms of Search and Destroy, Artillery, Us and Them, and War. We thought of the earth as an inert object, something we could antiseptically—and nobly—purify of disease. In those days I would walk out into the orchard with Paraquat, that dioxin-contaminated base for Agent Orange, in my back-pack sprayer. Throughout Vietnam, young Americans were thrashing through jungles and bare, leafless, yellow rice-paddies, drinking the contaminated water. As the sun poured down through my yellow hair like the clear notes of a bell, I would spray it over our own soil. In one day, the weeds would be dead and white, as if they had stood out through two years of snow and sun and rain. This black, oily liquid would spill over my hands and down my back, soaking the fifties Indian sweater with the green and gold pheasants on the pockets that my mother no longer cared to wear and had handed down to me. I had to throw it away.

DDT

"It kills weeds not people. You could drink it. You could drink it straight out of the bottle. They just put the warnings on it to protect themselves. Hal fed DDT to his sheep for a month, more and more every day, until at the end of the month they were getting nearly two pounds a day—of DDT. God, those animals grew strong! They were clean and strong—without worms or any other thing. So then he had the meat tested—less chemical residue than any other meat on the market!"

The Ancient Sea

IN THE POOLS of river water that collected on the benchland soil as the water poured out of the hydrants in the spring, there would often be worms—a foot long or more, and white, as thin as horsehairs, twining around each other as the light caught the water and filled it. In that lens I would look back millions of years into time.

Break Up

Bᴜᴛ ᴍʏ father's hands were not large enough to hold any of this world. All through the year, all spring and summer, they tried to get a grip on the air, but once the sky opened suddenly at the end of August and fall was upon us, when the windfall apples lay in the grass under the trees and the air smelled like mildew and snow, those hands were still empty—although with the slugs, the silver trails of the slugs, and the scent of apples filling the air, you would think even the stars should be dancing, despite the growing cold. Above us all, the mountains stared down over our shoulders, shifting through their seasons in a dance with snow and light.

Suddenly it would be spring again: the snow would lift and the trees, no longer black in the thin winter light, would blow into green flame—all before we had a chance to catch our breath. Above the farm the dry slopes of Fairview Mountain, eroded by flash floods into deep gullies of soapstone and shale, would break into the yellow fires of the balsam roots, hundreds of acres of cowpies and sunflowers under the blue air, that suddenly, out of nowhere, became blue and deep as the valley filled with dust and wind.

One spring we drove up into that dancing land of the sun. Colours were more clear in those years, more full of water and of dust. We had not yet been so completely trained to see with the eye of a camera, squashing depth and life to two dimensions of silver crystals arranging themselves upon paper at the breath of light: we were seeing with the physical eye. As they do every day, the mountain breezes were sinking off the mountain, late to surface from the shadows of dawn, colder than the deeps of the valley. In the blue Volkswagen we drove through them along the mountain's flank into those yellow fields. This was a country of air and the orchards were far below us, squares of blossoms, white apples, white apricots—bleached; ivory pears, and shadows of lipstick, rose-pink, for the peaches. We ate a simple lunch: a thermos of water that tasted of stale coffee, along with dry bread and the soft, punky apples of spring: Winesaps, with their strange flavour of parsnips, or Kidneys, rusty-red, with the colour bleeding out of the skins and into the flesh. For years I wondered every spring why we never went back there to those black fir gullies and sunlit slopes, but I never thought to ask.

If you were to dig down through the soapy yellow volcanic ash below the topsoil, and then down to the black splintered basalt of the dreaming earth that in our shared lives is our memory—with an eagle soaring far overhead in the pale gasses of the spring sky, screaming—you would find I had somehow learned, without the words or gestures to express it, "we had long before left the protection of the gods in that house." The night above us was empty and cold. It was not a liberating cold, but a cold that knocked you between the shoulder blades and sent you crumpled on your knees to the ground, and you were afraid to move.

The Wolves at Evelyn

MY MOTHER learned cold in the way you can only learn it when you are young. When she was twelve, with tight braids in her silver-blonde hair, they left Mission, where my grandfather had worked as an electrician on the dam at Stave Lake through both the Depression and the Second World War, and went seven hundred and fifty miles north through the jackpine and mud to a farm under the Evelyn Glacier west of Smithers. The farm was a group of run-down cabins sinking slowly into a spring. The bottom logs had already rotted away. Every winter day there—half the year—my mother would walk two miles through the birch forests, in the dark, to catch the sleigh that would take her the other ten miles to school. There would be wolves, pacing along with her step by step, a hundred feet away among the trees. In the afternoon they would wait for her again. Once again it would be dark, and the stars and the Northern Lights would flood above her, like something that should be loved. But in that country, where even the summer smells of snow, where the grass is thin and sparse, she learned to walk very fast and never look to her sides.

Hardboard

My GRANDPARENTS were city people, from Breslau—a city that no longer exists on any map. Its only life is as a dim grey memory of a faded, dusty photograph that hung against the hardboard of a dark front room, in the floodplain of the Similkameen River, in Canada. Now the dumps of the continent are filling up with hardboard, ripped out of houses wherever it is found, because no nail can be driven into it that will not soon be pushed back out; and now Breslau is my memory of a photograph, not my grandparents' memory of a living city.

My grandfather fled because he was a communist. After the war all the other Germans there fled as well, in front of the Russians. And after the war my grandparents fled too, fled again, fled from the Bomb, packed up and moved to their farm below the glacier and the clouds it drew darkly out of the living air, in the north of British Columbia, so far from the world, where they cleared the bush with an axe, a pry-bar and a horse, eighteen hours a day—land first cleared by the Norwegians in 1909, and then abandoned, land that had to be cleared again.

My grandfather bought one hundred and fifteen acres of farm. Seven years later he sold five hundred and ten acres. All cleared by hand.

Boiled Lungs

WHENEVER I grumbled about the porridge my mother pushed in front of us, she would tell me how, when her parents killed a pig, they would all damn well eat it, from its ears to its flinty hooves, like chicken scratch, from its liver to its lungs. "Pigs' lungs are grey," she would insist. "They taste like tough sponge rubber."

Every winter night the small girl would walk out of the house at sixty below, against the wind, her head bent down under the living stars so that she saw only the blue snow before her, two hundred yards through the drifts to her cabin, out in the darkness. There she slept with a fire that warmed only the upper three feet of the room and died out after an hour. On an empty stomach, she would lie there in self-hate, trying to sleep, while all around her the air turned to ice, like the thought that lives permanently in the eye of a wolf and never makes it back to the brain.

In the morning, under the same stars, she would reverse the trip, looking into the blue wells of her footsteps, the stumbling stains she had left in the snow the night before, only to face the same lung on her plate—except that now it was cold, not warm, and even further than it was the night before from a pig's hot breath.

From such a perspective, with the winter air sinking off the glacier all summer and over the house, and through the house, and even settling among the stems of the grass where the thin sun could not get at it, and chilling the feet, it is no wonder that mountains provide for her no self-liberating distance. Only in July did that house of dark, rotting logs stand for a few weeks out of the mountain's shadow. All summer long the winter cold locked in her bones, while the air around her, thinned with the scant heat, stiffened her, and year by year, under that same cold, her father turned hard with anger and fatigue. The old gods of blood demand death and submission to the earth, and they will have it through the only open channel, through work, or even war, if that is how they must gain access to the light.

The Inheritors of the Earth

I HAVE THOUGHT that the high southern slopes of light and heat would be a release, a slow pleasure to be sipped, like dandelion wine, in the winter of the heart, but it won't hold up: children have small need or patience for the dreams of adults and at best understand little of them. And I have thought that the ants—after all, to my mother who grew up in the sterile north, they were exotic, tropical, superfluous—would make the difference: they cover the entire dry gopher-mounded slope with the neural nets of a dreaming mind, and I have thought if nothing else they should make the difference, but even those dry bees of the earth cannot do that to the frozen memory, although they can to the child, and did for me. In these late years of the earth I think of them often, clinging to the soil there, high in the wind.

In a narrow field between the mock-orange and the river at Brushy Bottom, all through the summer of 1983, the ants surrounded me, and crawled over me. Every peach tree I grafted, as my head pounded from the sun, shed ants as I sliced into its bark with my knife. All around me there were ants: through the cactus and bunchgrass, through my chest-high trees, and up into the brown, sticky twigs of the birches along the dike, tossing their leaves like women threshing grain out of fish scales whenever the wind, with its perfume of purple-backed martins and willows, rose off the face of the river. The ants

filled two acres of field. At no point was there a distance of
more than five inches, in any direction, between one ant
and another. Their hill was in the mock-orange, that white-
flowered, nectarless wild rose. The nest was three feet tall, and
four feet through at the base, a loose jumble of fir needles and
gravel and sawdust. All summer I worked in that colony, sharing in its dreamings, but in the spring, as the cat-piss of the cy-
anide began again to evaporate off the new shoots of the
peaches—tiny, red with the cold—I discovered that the ants,
with nothing else to eat, were chewing through the grafts, to
collect the scraps of crystallized sap that had gathered there
the summer before. That afternoon I bought a can of Diazinon
crystals, a maggot-killer, for onions, and sprinkled the con-
tents over the hill. The ants carried the sweet-smelling grains,
small cubes of milky light, into their nest, where they decom-
posed into a gas, and fumigated them all. I betrayed myself. I
should have let them have the trees. The winter had taken the
rest: freakish, windy, and cold.

When I think back to those ants streaming over the dry,
cow-shit stained slopes of Kobau mountain it is like opening a
door and having the sun pour in when all that I thought was
out there was rain, clouds low along the hills, the weeds in the
garden all black and limp and sodden a few days before the fall
moon, and the first snow, when the mind clears suddenly and
forgets all about the sun. At that point, with such a memory of
a year behind it, the mind, the leaf-like human thought, the
bird dream, the grain of light, does not need the sun, but has
its own light, as yet undistilled. It's like opening a door and
finding the light there already distilled and warm, as if you
were looking into something a hundred years ago when on the
valley bottom the bunchgrass was as high as a horse, and no-
one had yet brought their gods to this land. The only god was
Coyote, the trickster, the fool loping wild through the grass,
chasing rabbits and talking in barks and squeaks.

2

THE SACRIFICIAL WORLD

Scapegoats

"THE FIRST TIME I tried to mow the orchard, the front of the tractor smashed down one way, I flew off the back another way, the tractor smashed to a sudden halt and stalled, and all around me the grass swayed—moving—it was pigs! From the neighbour! Running and squealing into the grass. And they were vicious too! I tracked them through these weeds. They had a whole bunch of mud-holes, and all day there they would lie in the cool shade.

"I didn't just find pigs there either. I got the tractor going again after the trouble, and I hadn't gone fifty feet, when the front of the tractor lurched up before me, right into the sky. Jesus Christ, I thought. You know, I'd run up on a disc-harrow that had been left there and the weeds had covered it. Ya, but both the tires were flat on the tractor. So when I got those fixed and had dragged the disc out, I started in again. I hadn't gone ten feet when the tractor heaved up again, bang! and it wouldn't go. Run up onto a harrow that had been behind that disc! All four tires were flat. And this was getting expensive too, you know! We kept calcium chloride in the tires, as weight—to keep it stable you know—so it was a big mess. You might think it's funny or wonder how I didn't see these things, but in that mess you couldn't see a thing. After all, I didn't pay much for the place. It was the most run-down orchard in the country. I sold the disc for five bucks. The harrow

I kept. I already had a disc. The neighbour had pigs and goats and horses. He was the janitor of the school. You know. The animals were really his wife's idea, so he didn't want anything to do with them, he just let them wander wherever they liked!"

Those were not the last pigs on that farm, but where they were wild, their descendents had a small, extremely muddy, sty beside the toolshed. There they squealed, spent their days lying on the shreds of straw buried in the mud, and ran us down when we went in with the water. As they pushed us about, water slopped out of the buckets and caught in the wind; when we went in with shovels to try to muck things out they bit our legs.

They were small when they came, pink and clean, with bright white eyes and sharp teeth. Their teeth were white as well, like the core of an apple split open between the hands and before it browns with the air. I was six years old and they scared me with their roughness.

To feed them we had the bottom half of an old dormant-oil barrel propped up on two crumbling cinderblocks. It had been cut by a cold chisel and a hammer, by hand. Its edges were jagged and black, and often drew blood from our wrists.

Dormant-oil is a thin petroleum oil, laced with sulfur. Under the eggshell light of the spring sun, when the chickens begin again to scratch through the gravel for seeds and worms, the light ruffling their feathers and sitting like small droplets of water in their eyes, the insects suffocate within their dormant-oil encased shells. If they are strong enough to push out into the harsh gasses of the air, their breathing holes clog and they still suffocate.

In an old, cut-off dormant-oil barrel, we boiled our cull potatoes by the sackful. Snapped at by frost, black-cored with the cold, soft and wrinkled, the potatoes gave off a hot steam—sweet, almost fermented, and pure—the scent of night. It rose from our pigweed-stubbled garden straight up to the stars. The stars hung just over the roof of the house. Occasionally one would be snagged by the fine black tips of the elms along the edge of the bank and would burst in a great orange snap of sparks, like seeds spat off the head of a dandelion by the breath. The stew we were stirring was the same swill of cow's heads, lice, turnip tops and potato peels fed to the inmates of Buchenwald: *Eintopf*, soldier's stew, whatever you have, throw it into the pot, eat it with black bread. My father ate it, touring the bunkers and gun-placements dug into the pastures along the Rhine, twelve years old. Never, he said, had anything tasted so good.

For the pigs we mixed in windfall apples with the cull potatoes, all dumped into that oil barrel with the scraps from the kitchen and the smoke from the kitchen garbage that we burnt right outside the slats of the pen. We'd soak it with a cupful of diesel fuel to get it going in that wind, with a few large wet flakes of snow condensing out of the air suddenly right before us and melting again, almost immediately, when they hit the dark soil. The garbage burned black and rank, and from it the eyes of those pigs were red and swollen and full of pus.

We'd stand there at dusk, on the wobbly ends of old, half-rotten apple boxes, stirring that soup with long-handled garden hoes. In the wind and the smoke from the fire under the barrel, choking and shivering at the same time, we'd try to maintain our balance as the nails slowly pulled loose from the wood and the boxes collapsed under us. Once the stew was cooked we'd shovel it into buckets and carry it to those pigs. They'd squeal and smash their heads into the side of the pen and into each other as we came close and the wind carried that scent towards them, where they stood almost knee-deep in half-frozen muck.

Sometimes my brother would run around the back of the shed, up the stack of orchard ladders leaning against it there, and over the roof. While the pigs were diverted and half-sleepy with food, he'd slide on the seat of his pants down the rough plywood roof, through the pen, and out, leaping the fence. The one time I tried that trick I didn't land running—he always did. Before they let me go, the pigs smashed me into the rough-barked jackpine, once, hard, in the ribs, knocking out my breath, squealing with delight, jabbing my feet with their sharp hooves. After that I was content to freeze there over the barrel, sparks from the fire streaming away behind me into the night, the stars as cold and clear as stones above me, while my brother moved through the pigs and the mud like a shadow or a condensation of the darkness inside a stone.

Golden Corn

As I was picking the dried corn in my garden a few days ago and tossing it into the rusty bowl of the wheelbarrow, I was suddenly breathing that fall air when I was six years old. Every night after pruning and just before dark we would go out into the cornfield, and as the night fell over us we would pick the cobs into boxes for the pigs. With stiff fingers sliced by the sharp dry leaves, we loaded the boxes onto a pallet on the back of the tractor and rode home, shaking in the noise and stink of diesel and grease. The air would surge cold through my lungs and my eyes would clear. It is a rustling memory, a memory of crisp leaves and must. In the headlights of the tractor, the ears of corn were like ancient, beaten gold. My fingers would be so cold they could hardly grasp the cobs, but they did—ice clutching ice.

When the pigs were sold, my father came home from the stockyard in Kamloops and showed me three crisp 100 dollar bills. He laughed out loud, pulled a beer out of the fridge, and sat at the arborite table, the money spread out before him. I thought we were millionaires. Those bills were like stamps from Rwanda, or Qatar—exotic plumage, charged with power. They were like fall leaves off the sumacs, glistening with rain, plastered with the rain against the smooth moth-grey rocks of the hillside below the house, the colour draining out of them rapidly before my eyes. Still, it mustn't have been worth it, for there were never pigs on that farm again. We became fruit-growers only—specialists, internationalists. I missed those pigs a lot and did not understand why, and tried for years in my dreams to regain that time, to relive the fluid nature of the darkness, for that darkness was alive. But only rarely did that time return.

A Chicken Coop

HERE A SNATCH of Vivaldi, there the mechanical stresses within a diesel engine, there my father's Swiss method of boiling potatoes in the radiator of the tractor as he worked the fields: for us, culture was like a chicken coop—banged together by hand out of a few worn scraps. By throwing away his Goethe and his Bach, my father could breathe the raw, radioactive light of the pines, yet that ability to breathe the hot light without attaching words to it, one of the most complex of the logical crystals of European culture, is also a point of silence and worldlessness. As I was growing out of childhood I could look at the mountains, and could feel within me the snow sift through the black firs on the volcanic core of Crater Mountain and the Ashnola cliffs, and could taste it—profound knowledge, and worth fighting for—but I could not act upon it, for I had not yet learned to turn away.

With his first money earned in this country, my father bought a shortwave radio to listen to classical concerts from New York. When he married he budgeted $50 a month for photographic supplies. Neither lasted long. Although of an unparalleled fascination, for within it lay the secrets of entrance into the greater world, all through my childhood the radio sat in the basement, unused. The photographic papers and chemicals were stored in unused wooden strawberry crates in the attic. What remained were the trees, writhing, like sagebrush,

out of the shale and the desert loam. The ancient, hieratic ve-
neer of European civilization had been stripped off, and the
old gods of earth and river and blood and stone, and the slow
peat-smoke god of dark winter beer, had stepped forward, out
of the wilderness where they had survived within the very
things of this world; the pines and larches and the summer sky
lapping overhead at the peaks of the mountains like the small
wavelets at the shore of a river stilling out of a deep, white-
muscled current.

There is only one history.

Politics and Pipesmoke

"LISTEN, IF MY ten-year-old kid can hoe my trees or spread fertilizer under them out of a goddamn paper sack, there's no challenge in it for me. Business, that's what has to interest someone who's thirty-five years old, or you won't survive!" It was thrown out as a challenge. My grandfather would sit there across the room, under the juniper-wood lamp he'd made by hand, his Confucius and Marx on the shelf beside him. He'd take a long draw on his pipe, and slowly and in his deep, measured voice, with that reedy, flattened, North German accent that sounded first of tobacco but then behind it of the marshes and herring and places of the Baltic, would begin again to explain how a man could gain a life from such work—the only true value was what you could make with your own two hands. Then he would draw again on the pipe, slowly, measuredly, his eyes sparkling. But my father was not yet ready for that challenge.

The mistakes we make in our lives are the ones we repeat over and over. They have a strange attraction for us. We need them to maintain the fictions—visions, dreams, exultations— that we use to drag ourselves into the future and to divorce ourselves from the past. Everything clamours for us. Sometimes in weariness our faces go slack and lifeless: we have forgotten our future and are too stubborn or frightened to reinvent it.

When we were out working in the orchard, in the dancing fall wind that so easily draws more heat from the body than the steel blue air of winter, I would shiver in my thin socks and torn gumboots. "Well, if you are cold," my father would say, patiently and impatiently at the same time, "if you are cold, then jump up and down, kick your legs out, sideways, jump, eh, and slap your arms hard, harder, right against your shoulders. Keep doing it. Do it for two minutes. You will be warm then. I learned that in the camp during the War. Do it. Hard! No, harder!"

All this time, my mother would be in the house, fussing over the stove, looking out the calcium-pitted, white windows into the grey and unfocused cold. And while she was in there, trying to reclaim a life for herself from time, we were out in the cold, reliving the Second World War and the chill of the German sky at night, fog seeping right through the weave of our clothes.

We were lost in the world.

3
THE ETERNAL WAR

Night Raids

FOR THE FIRST years of his marriage in that white house above
the willow and alder scrub of the wetlands—the old oxbows—
of the Similkameen, my father would often wake up screaming
with nightmares of the bombings of Rastadt that he ran
through as a boy. Sick and pregnant, fighting to bring forth
children from her knotted womb, night after night my mother
pushed herself from sleep to run around the edge of the bed to
comfort him there, where he crouched, sweating, on the cold
linoleum, in the dust. Then he'd wake up fully and in a rage
burst out into the lurching, shivering house, and pour himself
a drink. My mother could see him there, through the crack of
the open door, a black shape staring out at the elms as they
writhed like snakes in the leaden moonlight. She'd lie there
awake and watch him shake, and then pour the liquor quickly
down his throat like a stab of fire, as the trees rose up and clattered against each other in a sudden flash of wind. Then, and
as suddenly, and as impulsively, his skin cold and grey, he'd
step away from the window and walk back to bed and collapse
into it, and cry. Night after night my mother forced herself to
stay awake and listen. In that half-sleep at two a.m., with the
planes diving down at my father out of the blue sky and the
cobbled street lifting up beneath him, to flick him off, intently
and casually at the same time, the way a man might crush a
louse in the seams of his jacket, every minute became a half-

hour, and the darkness throbbed visibly around the bed.

In that darkness their low voices eased out into the air, until over the hours they filled the house, like a form of electricity, like a giant bird, taking shape, finally spreading out its wings —the house splintering around them—and lifting up into the night. Then it would be dawn and they'd try to sleep, for half an hour maybe, until my father stumbled off to work, until my brother and I too stepped, bewildered and afraid, out of our dreams.

Education Under Fire

THE SCHOOL IN my father's village had been shelled early in the war by the French from across the Rhine. It was the only building in town that was hit, and it was completely destroyed. This was my father's story, and there was none more important. Not only did my mother hear this story, but every visitor that came to our house heard it, once the beer had begun to thin my father's blood and clear his eyes.

"So, one day we were going in to Rastadt, to school. All we had to eat was beer. There was nothing to eat, just nothing, but for a couple of *pfennigs* you could get a litre of beer, so Richard and I, we would do that. Go down there by the train station and get some beer. We were just kids, you know.

"And then we'd get on the train. Well, one day the British bombed Rastadt, the Industrial Section—flattened it right to the ground. That was the day before. On the next day, the day after that, we were going in to school on the train, and it was going slow, too, 'cause the tracks were all busted up. We were all on the train, all of us kids from Kuppenheim, and the other villages, in the second grade. As we got close to Rastadt, there was an alarm, an air-raid siren, the planes were coming. So the conductor came through the train then. He said when we get to Rastadt we all have to go down right away into the shelter that was in the basement, under the station, and we would

have to hurry, and go down as soon as the train got into the
station.

"We were just kids though, they wanted to protect us. Ya.
So as the train was slowing down in the suburbs, before it got
downtown in Rastadt, I said to Richard, I don't know why, I
guess it's just one of those crazy things you do sometimes,
'why don't we jump off the train before the station, at the next
stop, and go up into the industrial area and see where they
bombed yesterday? And we can see the planes.' Then I said,
'you don't want to go into the shelter, do you?' and Richard
said 'no,' so we did that, you know, got off the train and went
up into the bombed-out area. It was still smoky and burning.
It was dangerous, I guess, really, a dangerous place. And we
looked at all the factories, *Bayrische Motor Werke, Bayerwerke, Sie-
mens*. I can still see those signs there burning. It was a bright
clear day. It was just in the middle of the morning. It was hot
and blue. None of us, you know, expected the planes to bomb
the town again. What for? They had just bombed it the day
before. Everyone was just being safe, because of the kids.

"So we were up there and Richard and I heard the planes
coming. We saw them, four of them, and then four more, and
four more, as far as you could see, with the ak-ak, the flak
bursting among them, little white puffs. Their engines droned,
right in the air. We thought they were just passing over, going
somewhere else, to the east. But we saw the bombs then. They
fell in the light like silver, glittering and bright. They looked so
pretty. But they weren't pretty, of course, falling there, for we
saw the whole town blow up down below us. When we got
back down to the train station we went to see what happened,
they were just pouring the lye on all our schoolchums, they
were all dead, all those guys we went to school with. Kids. The
British had been aiming at the train station, and they all suffo-
cated in the shelter. Ya. Those were terrible times, hard times.

"I remember another time, Richard and I, we used to go to
Rastadt—to see his grandmother. Richard had just got a bi-
cycle from his father, brand new, so I borrowed one from

somebody, I can't remember who, I don't remember who, there weren't many bicycles, but that doesn't matter now, it's not important, so we said well why don't we go in and see Oma—see Grandma. So we do that, we bike all the way in to Rastadt, and we go to her apartment. There's food rationing then you know, and not much extra to eat, just potatoes and onions, and sometimes maybe cottage cheese that you can make in a cloth hanging from the ceiling in the kitchen. The whey drips out through the cloth as the cheese curdles, and you can drink that too, and we did that. Ya, it didn't taste so good though. She didn't have enough to eat, I'm sure, but Richard's grandma, she would always have something there for us to eat. Something she'd baked. You know, cake maybe, or some kind of sour oat and plum pudding, 'cause she could not get much sugar. That was all for the soldiers.

"Well, there we are there when the sirens go off, and the planes are coming. So everybody's screaming and shouting, and Richard's grandmother gets us to go down into the basement with everybody else in the building. There it was dark and wet and cold. The whole building above us fell down and I thought we were dead. I thought we would never get out. It's horrible.

"I learned too much about people down there. Some people are saints and some are just shit. Even when you're a kid, you're nine years old, you understand that. We were down there for two days, in the dark. There wasn't much air, and if you had to shit or piss you had to do it in the corner, and everybody would know. It would stink. Some people give you everything they have because they know you're just a kid—and some people push you in the chest, and whine, and scream, but you're just a kid and you're scared. That's where I got tough. When they finally dug us out it was two days later. The idiots came in from the side! They didn't even use the emergency exit that had been put there just in case we got bombed in! When we came out of there it took half an hour before I could see. Even though it was a foggy day it was just too bright. I could see a little bit, a splash of colour, part of a building or something, but it didn't last, it didn't fit together into anything. But then I could see again.

"From then on I told myself I'd never again get myself trapped. If all the people were running one way, I'd run the other way. It's safer to go somewhere and be by yourself. You can take care of yourself. If you go where everybody else is going, that's the worst place to go. Because you're there you have to do what they do, and they're just stupid. You have to do things on your own. I was just a kid but I knew that. I did that, from then on. I'd run outside, anything but go down there again. Once there was a guard yelling at us: Go down into the basement! So I ran down the hall and jumped through the window that was at the end of the hall, to get away from the guard. I had cuts all over my face and hands from that glass, little cuts, and the blood ran down my face. I just ran away from there. And the bombs blowing up behind me in the street. You don't forget that. When you're young, you have determination. The most important thing is just to live."

This is the one detail he cares to relate, for his memory, like a tree growing on a high, windswept ridge, on one side drunk on oxygen and on the other with horizontal ideas of gravity, works only through those anecdotes he has brought up over and over and chewed and re-swallowed. The rest has been dismissed and so does not surface, though it is his life. It is there somehow, in the way he holds his pale, small hands before himself as if they were not his; it is there in his nervous laughter, and in the almost drunken dislocation between his thoughts, the frenzy with which they all pile on top of each other, coalescing, reforming, like the nightmares of Johannes Grimm after ten years of collecting folk stories, with their wild, interchangeable motifs, that mean nothing. When I told him, "No, the Grimm Brothers collected the complex living stories of the German peasants and recorded the entire German language, living stories, not book-learned stories but what men used in the wild, as they were dying out, being absorbed into a

new bureaucratic culture," and when I said they recorded the
German mind, the voice of its god before it fell into time, like a
pile of useless stones, he only laughed and said, "No, no, those
are children's stories that they told." And he was right.

I think my mother has never heard these living nightmares
of my father, and with all the strength of a candle cupped between the hands to shelter it from the wind, he has tried to kill
them. They are weeds. They burst up into his soil, and drain
all the light so no other thought can grow. Kochia, Russian
thistle, knapweed, pigweed—those Russian weeds that came
over to this country from grain shipped out from the German
farms of the Ukraine, before the wars that set us free and
ruined us.

Pathfinding

WHILE MY MOTHER was in the house, beneath that attic of loose shavings and between the skittering, mice-filled walls, fighting to provide some centre of care and gentleness to the totally random rhythms of despair and elation that are the life of a farm—which so quickly explode into anger—my father was out trying to build on this soil a country he could live in; and we, my brother and I, by one of the strange twists of the mind as it looks out of the skull into the harsh atmosphere of sun and stone, unable to take in that war of matter and light, were struggling to remake, in my father's image, the Hitler boy camps in the Black Forest.

In camp my father learned that compassion, even compassion for the self, was without value, that the body was a machine, that love was only an animal instinct, and that government was out to destroy us. It was there that he learned that we were virtuous and pure and through our work with the soil, we were the rulers of men, and he trained us in it, with work. This was a strange, exotic religion. This was not the *Hitler Jugend* proper. It was a sort of preparatory camp for the younger boys, ten years old to twelve years old. "We were selected," said my father, "by our grades in school. The top two boys in every class got to go. It was a great honour to be chosen like that. You have no idea. I was weak in trigonometry and I needed to do well in my exam or I couldn't go. I couldn't understand the stupid stuff. So they crammed it into me, and I still hate it to this day, but I learned it. So I went there too.

"In the camp we learned everything you could think of: how to make a bed, you know to military standards, and if we didn't get it right, or didn't get anything right, we had to keep remaking it over and over until we did. Everything we did we learned something.

"We had a lot of fun. Hebrew! of all things, ya!, always what you'd need as an officer, how to take apart a rifle and clean it, and jumble all the parts together, and put the rifle back together, and then in the dark, and trigonometry, gun trajectories and stuff, how to hammer with the left hand, how to write with the left hand—how to do everything with the left hand. So I can do everything with both hands. I learned that there. And we learned why there was a war. We were old enough to be told that. So they told us. That made us very proud. It was business, big business you know, international finance and manufacturing: they were at war against us, against the man who just wanted to live on his own with the earth and take at last what he deserved from it, because he lived with it. And the stupid church. And there was all sorts of other shit, all the time, all sorts of propaganda, Hitler this and *Heil Hitler* that, and we learned about Jews too. Every morning, first thing, before we ate, we had to run naked two miles through the forest, down to a creek. It didn't matter if there was snow on the ground either. We had to wash, right in the creek.

"Ya, Adolf Hitler was born on April 20, 1889, in Braunau-am-Inn. We learned that. Useless shit, eh. But it was very important.

"We would have bread and that black army sausage. We learned how to identify planes, whose they were, and what they were doing, and about all the different kinds of weapons. I was in a glider. They were teaching us to fly, 'cause they needed pilots. I crashed the damn thing into the ground, nearly killed myself. It was so funny.

"One day I was out in the forest. It was another exercise

you know, everything was an exercise, on my own, following the compass. Well, I heard the planes go over and when I got back to the camp, the whole place was blown all to bits, pieces of bodies lying around everywhere, and nothing left, and blood over everything, and fire and stink. There was nobody there left to tell me what to do, so I just turned and walked home, twenty kilometres. I didn't see anybody. Of course I wasn't supposed to go, but so what. There was nothing. I walked all night and then I got home to Mama. We didn't have any food but at least I was home. And it was a good thing I came home too, because Mama was all alone in that house, the other kids were all up at Pforzheim and Gaggenau, away from the Rhine, where it was safe, and she needed someone to help her. I stayed there through everything."

Coming to Life

IT WAS ALL so long ago. We no longer have the orchard now; its memories have totally evaporated from my mind. To find them, I have to remake them. I have to stare hard at objects until I suddenly see them. They spring up out of the air before me, just where I had thought they were all along, where I thought I had lost them, but with one crucial difference: they are alive.

4
THE WINTER CAMPAIGN

Vanishing into the Land

Summer, the one season for which this valley is famous, is the one season that never stuck with me. It was all work in the summer, with nothing of the self to break the work and so make it dance with life. During the summers I was lost in a physical trance. For whole hours at a time I would not be there. I would be work. I would be the trees. I would be the air. When we walked down the driveway in the steel heat the air would ripple around us like the exhaust of a blast furnace. We moved through the trees silently and alone. All around us the trees would be pumping out water into their leaves and from their leaves into the air, as fast as they could draw it out of the soil, to keep themselves from bursting into sudden yellow and smokeless flame. All through the summers we watched my father out spraying with that foolish old sprayer. Like a helicopter, it needed two hours of repair for every two hours of work, but then it would blow the spray out in such volume and at such pressure that the trees streamed with white rain for five minutes after it had passed, and the whole air stank, sharp, and the white, star-like fan of spray rose forty feet above the trees. The spray would drift a hundred feet, in slow motion, through the rows. It smelled of ashes and weeds and mildew and paint and death, yet for me it is the smell of life, the smell of the farm. When I walk into that smell today, anywhere, it makes me stagger and my head throbs, but at the same time it makes me remember those days when life was so intense, lived among the mosquitoes and dandelions at double speed—physical, because there was nothing to think about, and no language to think about it with, and deliberate. It is a smell that is very difficult to wash from the hands.

A Caged Bull

THAT OLD, red-rusted Hardy was pumped dry by three four-inch pistons of frozen steel. Black and greasy, they were driven by the power-take-off, a metal rod green with grease, revolving at 540 rpm between the sprayer and the tractor. It was an old sprayer though, and lacked a valve to release the pressure back into the tank when the nozzles were closed. Its twin didn't have one either. Picked up for parts from the weeds behind a prop pile in Penticton, it sat in its pool of grease and flakes of old, red lead paint, slowly dissolving into the mud floor of the shed. Without a pressure-relief valve, when you turned around the end tree of a row and started down the next, the whole system would leap like a striking rattler up to 500 psi and the tractor would shake like a caged bull, tilting first on one rear wheel and then on the other.

In June I'd be standing at the top of my ladder, thinning. By then, the apple trees would have already aborted the poorest fruit, apples with only one fertile seed or none at all. With the aborted apples lying on the ground beneath me, small and yellow, like oozings of wax, or sickly dead insects, I'd thin out the ones eaten by bugs or scabbed by wind. As I spat the small, hard fruits into the grass with my fingers, in the pears only a few rows away the pistons hammered and the sheet metal of the sprayer shook and snapped like a hurricane. As always, in those years, the years of rust, I did not understand

what it meant. I did not understand that there are conse-
quences to our actions, that what happens in our physical
earth reverberates through time and changes the dimensions
of space. I did not know then that time and space do not differ,
and that we create them. The distance between action and
consciousness is vast.

Air War

THE SPRAY SPEWED out of two half-moons of nozzles at the rear of the Hardy, blown high above the trees by the whine of a fan that would nearly blow you flat to the dandelions and plantain if you walked past it. It sounded like one of those Messerschmidt 109's fighting those hopeless battles over Rostov in 1942. It sat at the back of a bell-shaped metal housing, and was covered with a coarse steel mesh, like a hockey mask. While the pump was powered by the tractor, the fan was driven by its own engine—a deafening 12 hp air-cooled Wisconsin.

My unspoken childhood: in the winter advance the Germans sent patrols right into the suburbs of Moscow; beaten back by workers pouring out of the factories, armed only with their pipe-wrenches, that was as far as they got. That was my war. That winter the Germans, their tanks and trucks seized up with cold, spent entire days at sixty below digging the roads out of four- and six-foot drifts, by hand, so that under the acid cover of night, at three in the afternoon, they could pull back through the bare birch forests the distance they had dug during the day. All around them the tree trunks were snapping from the cold, and through those trees the Russians, dressed in white parkas, on skis, harried them, like wolves.

The Russians held close to the earth, and the earth saved them. For the Germans, however, the helplessness and abandonment was the end of a dream—the end of the desperate hope that this evil would come out alright—and the loss of the earth. That was the winter I relived over and over in all the years of my childhood. That was the winter Hitler held the Germans to their lines, damn the costs. But the earth is not so easily held by force. The next year he was in a frenzy, dissipated his attack and forbade any retreat into the shelter of the earth. That defeat was the bedrock of my life—no matter how my father tried to shelter me from it. We live under an open sky. There is no shelter.

In the spring, when Rostov could have been taken without a fight, it fell only at heavy cost, and Stalingrad drained every reserve of the Southern Front as division after division drove themselves against it, and were blown up house by house. Night after night, day after day, as I moved through my childhood, the Luftwaffe was destroyed, dive-bombing the deep, narrow canyons leading into the river. Their engines roared; pure gasoline whined through the veins of the pilots as they pitched down and dropped their bombs into the throat of the earth; and the earth hardly rippled under the assault, only tossed in her sleep. In the end, the German headquarters was in the basement of a bombed-out building, sixty men lying in blankets on a concrete floor. The earth had defeated them for their pretensions over her power and for fighting in her name.

All summer I would hear that sound screaming out of the fan of the sprayer, and the sound of the trucks bouncing over the muddy, rutted roads in the hammering of the sheet steel of the sides of the sprayer, but I was just a kid and did not know what that meant. Even today, in the year of water evaporating from the driftwood on the silver gravel bar of the river, with the trees streaming directly out of the pores of the gravel into the air—the earth's sweat—I do not know how it is going to come for me, nor when, nor how I shall break with that slow sentence spilled out of the clouds. It has not, however, left me totally alone and helpless on this empty earth, because I know when it got my father, and I know how: in the blue-grey Feb-

ruary of 1957 my brother was born, and was given the name
Hans, my father's. It was a prophetic choice: he is so similar to
my father in thought and body—propelling himself forward
with his shoulders when walking—that they are almost exten-
sions of the same self. Some ancestor stares out through their
blue eyes together from its life of glaciers and shamans and
fear.

Rock

WHEN THOSE ancient German gods caught up with him, my
father was out doing the one and only job that he ever man-
aged to do over and over again, although with an ever-
increasing sense of hopelessness: he was out spraying in the
spring. But he was young then, confident—and thoughtless. A
family joke: "Rhenisch-head. Like a rock. Ty-pical." Then
you knock on the head in question with the knuckles, and it
thuds. This is a joke told by the wives.

He wasn't my father then. He was a young scarecrow with a
grin full of bad teeth. Suddenly this kid of fast cars and beer,
lonely, on the run, had found himself bogged-down in a do-
mesticity he didn't understand. All I know, and I have this
like a thirties wooden amulet of the sun, painted with thick,
lead-yellow paint, with garish, loud, black and red features, in
my fist, is that *once* he put it all together: on that spring day in
1957 he mixed in his tank, to save time, Zinc and Lime-
Sulphur, two incompatible chemicals, and they turned in-
stantly to cement.

In those days of broken English and nightmare, in that
empty country only ten years after the war, my father was
working the clay cliffs and benches above Penticton at Loch
Eden for Frank Laird. Years later, Mrs. Laird would turn
from her rock garden, a single flat sheet of glacier-scrubbed
schist, to paint oils of great feeling and subtlety and colour

but absolutely no craft or line or space—that hard Victorian work of building a country out of this unknown land, surviving among us in unfinished, unassimilated and unorchestrated forms.

When the darkness that stared him in the face, that drank the breath straight out of his mouth in that basement in Rastadt, faster than his lungs could puke it out, caught up to him again at last, finally got him to stand still in one place for a moment, he did the one thing, and only the one thing, that made up the rest of his life: he walked across the yard to the toolshed, picked up a hammer and a cold chisel, pulled one of those old rubber and paper cartridge spray masks from a nail on the wall, and in a cold, unthinking panic slipped into that tank. Four hours later Frank Laird dragged him out, unconscious. His skin was white with spray-dust. Through that dust it shone ghostly and blue.

Spraying is the only action in his life my father has been able to repeat. Look for any other and your hands will come up empty and then slip into your pockets and finger the keys and loose change there as you turn away. Yet every time he has sprayed since that year of frost and early rain he has grown violently sick. In the last two years that we had the farm he couldn't spray at all.

Those old orchards on the clay banks of Skaha Lake have now wandered into grass and sage, but they were once among the richest plantations of the Empire. They were steep, too—so steep that when the sprayer, full of two and a half tons of water on the first morning pass, in the yellow half-light, slipped sideways and caught a tree between itself and the Cat, my father simply shut the machine down and walked back through the perfume of the budding trees to the shed, pulled a pruning saw off a dark shelf, slipped back through the naked spring branches, and cut down the tree. He covered the sawdust up with a piece of sod, dragged the tree over to the burning pile, put the Cat into gear and sprayed the rest of the day. The sky over him was huge, and relentless, and blue.

That was my father then, on those cliffs above Penticton. A
kid with a hot car, a sick young wife, a red-cheeked hungry son
and another coming—swamped. A man who no longer exists.
He was simply burnt away by the sun and then caught up by
the wind and driven before it.

5
LIVING WINTER

Alone with the Land

WINTER HAS always been for me the season of greatest life. In the summers, when the air is parched and the hills have retreated deep into their cool cores, the tourists come for their images of paradise. For me that is the briefest time: the time of passage, the months of unending work. The winter continues, almost forever, cold and clear. The oxygen thickens in the air until it is almost water, and the earth belongs to the earth. There can be whole weeks without a single star. It is then, in the cold, that the mountains come into their own, and live, huge black animals crouching along the edges of the fields, their eyes bright.

By ripping out all its orchards for retirement homes and motels, Penticton has destroyed the dream that brought people here. But Penticton is just pain, a cancer. In Victorian and Edwardian times we colonized the wild land; now we colonize that Edwardian image—hoping for those old attitudes miraculously to animate us, both emulating and despising them with the same strength that we once did the land itself. So summer is the time of failure here, and winter, when we are with the earth, is the time of life: when you can walk out into the fields alone, and there is nobody there, when all has been stripped bare of pretense and thought, and can be touched, if not as physical objects, at least as a secret and miraculous fire.

Even in those years when we still had the farm, when we

were still a family together, when we were not yet driven into
ruin, when family was still more than a memory to us, I would
rarely sleep. Family and self and the farm were the same: all
our energy—all the energy we burned off together—had gone
into the land. I'd lie awake in that black room in the basement, the black widows and the crickets and the frogs all
around me, overwintering in the cracks in the concrete behind
the thin wood wall beside my bed. For one week each fall, and
then again in the spring, those frogs would sing all night from
their cracks. Then they would move out, either into the blackness of sleep or into the yellow fields of the sun, and I would
feel the seasons shift slowly around me, in my sleeplessness, in
the dark.

The Mushroom Beds

NEXT TO THE laundry tubs and under the kitchen my father grew mushrooms. He had carefully blended dirt and horse manure, had set both humidity and heat at exact levels, and on the night when the mushrooms were due to rise went down with Otto to watch. They sat down there in that hot, sweet air, their flashlight, shrouded with a red wool sock, glowing on a mushroom bed in front of them. They sat down there for hours, drinking out of a tall bottle of cheap whiskey and listening to the manure-sharp water drip onto the concrete. Pale in the long red shadows of the light, the mushrooms sprouted. They were so full of the dark that within two hours they were two inches tall. Then they collapsed onto the manure again, black, shrivelled skins. When my father came upstairs, Otto was laughing. "What's wrong?" my mother asked. "Dorothy, you've got to come down and see this," my father said weakly. So they trooped back down again. Except this time they didn't bother with the flashlight but switched on the naked white bulb overhead. The room looked dirty in that light, where no bright light had shone for months. "Here, Dorothy," said Otto, and passed my mother his glass. She sat it neatly, tidily, on the corner of one of the tables. "I don't get it," she said. "Toadstools," said my father. Toadstools! By the end of the next day he had the room emptied and washed clean.

In that room, I would lie awake. When I could bear the

blackness no longer I would clamber out of bed, onto the frozen, grey-painted concrete. By the back door, beside the sawdust burner, I would step barefoot into my gumboots, then out into the trees, and the stars.

The moonlight shone through that bitter, almost weightless wind of ice and sent long shadows through the branches, and I stepped through those shadows, as if I were threading my way through a deep unearthly forest, and up onto the gravel ridge that ran at an alluvial angle through the centre of the farm. There the trees were half-stunted with the poor soil, and I could get some air; and with the dog at my side, a black, rough-clawed shadow, I would run and run through the bitter, hard white snow. With each step, my footsteps would snap the crusts and a fine spray of ice would sift down into my boots. When I would get back inside, I would be cold, but my mind would be awake, and full of wind and moonlight, and I would sleep.

And all the time that I ran, the trees shifted past me, sudden black spirits, jumping up out of nowhere in the air. Even then—with my heart pounding and a wind blowing at me straight out of the rock itself and out of the starlight, as I lay in bed with small pieces of grit from the boots between my toes, I wanted to shake it all off—I was running somewhere, but it was some place to which I couldn't arrive by running, and here I am, at that place, my lungs heaving, sucking in oxygen, drunk on that cold—living it.

When I think back on that time it is that cold I remember, and how, with it, I nearly felt free.

Worship and Possession

TIME IS NOT the house of thought and succession I have made it out to be with my histories. History is a tool for organizing our social lives, to make the dead past live: ancestor worship. But in time itself the past lives, simply. It is a physical weight, adapted exactly to the body. It is the language of the body, speaking itself into completeness across space, forming a space that can give form to the random actions of life, to make them physical, to put all our thoughts into the language of the body, so that when we walk they move with us. It's not by words that the body forms the future, but by transforming its image of itself, outside of words. And just as Keremeos Creek changes colour every hour as the sky above it darkens with winter, and yet appears the whole time the colour of water, so my mother has never returned to Evelyn. When she says the word to herself she shivers. So she just doesn't say it.

We cannot escape our past.

6

THE DEMANDING DEAD

Machines

THIS IS A list of the machines we kept on the farm: one 75 hp water pump, one 50 hp water pump, three 3 hp water pumps, one three-ton truck, three Massey Ferguson 135 Diesel Tractors, one disc harrow, one harrow, one cultivator, one rotovator, one ditching plow, one rototiller, one 3-bottom plow, one antique Hardy Sprayer, one Hardy sprayer for parts, one Woods Co80 rotary mower, one spray gun, one Pak Tank weedsprayer with boom, one Solo backpack sprayer, one front-end bin fork, three rear bin-forks, one hydraulic top-link, one hydraulic pruning lift, one gas-welding outfit, one arc-welding outfit, one bench grinder, one skilsaw, one electric drill, two bench vises, one sub-soiler, one anvil, one tree-hole auger, one tree-planting machine, two trailers, one fertilizer spreader, one stone-boat, one chainsaw, one hydraulic pruner, one hydraulic saw, two pick-up trucks, one D3 cat, one sprinkler-moving tractor, one nursery digging plow, one asparagus grader, one five-ton truck.

These are the tools we kept on the farm: one complete set of Gray wrenches and sockets, two pipe wrenches, flints, pliers, one hand gas pump, one set Allen wrenches, one hand fence-post auger, one spark plug gapping tool, a dozen screwdrivers, an awl, a hammer, a sledge-hammer, grubhoes, two dozen garden hoes, asparagus knives, asparagus buckets, picking bags, buckets, onion hoes, short-handled shovels, long-handled shovels, pitchforks, sawdust forks, potato forks, saw-dust shovels, pruning clippers, hand clippers, budding knives, eight-foot pole pruners, ten-foot pole pruners, eight-foot pole saws, ten-foot pole saws, thinning shears, ring knives, tree-girdling knives, wire cutters, tin snips, bolt cutters, baling wire, ball-peen hammer, carpenter's hammers, adze, hacksaw, woodsaw, swede-saws, brace and bit, tap-and-die set, chains, come-alongs, block and tackle, a cement mixer, a gearpuller, grease guns, hose spray-nozzles, vice grips, flat files, round files, triangular files, sharpening stones, scythe stones, brush scythes, grass scythes, an insect screen, punches, a kerosene blowtorch, a battery charger, a voltage tester, eight-foot three-legged wooden ladders, ten-foot three-legged wooden ladders, extension ladders, boxes, a box-nailing machine, pallets, nails, binoculars, adding machines, bolts, sisal twine, polypropylene twine, pruning saws, a fruit pressure-tester, gopher prods, gopher-poisoning guns, gopher traps, a .30-30 Winchester rifle, a .22 rifle, a shotgun, crowbars, prybars, a hand-held post-hole auger, picks, axes, hatchets, a maximum-minimum thermometer, snowshoes, grafting knives, secateurs, a level, flints, cables, a box stapler, razors, hoses.

Trinkets of Power

MACHINERY IS THE death of farming. It breeds carelessness around trees. It demands that the efficiency of the machine become the efficiency of the farm. With machines, there is no entrance into the work—into the land: all you can enter is the machine itself. That can destroy you. Worse yet, young men, and boys even, approach machines as a bedrock. Machines offer us power. They are inefficient. They cost a lot of money and they do not get the work done. They are part of the religion of death, and they dazzle us.

Windbreaks

OUR HOUSE SAT above a sumac- and saskatoon-blotted alluvial bench, high gravel deposits left to us from the run-off of the last glaciers. In 1963, afraid that the Similkameen wind would shatter the glass right out of the window frames, my father planted Siberian elms as a windbreak. Today, Sally, the woman who now lives in that seasick house of surging, watery windows, would almost kill over those trees: each spring they erupt in a wind of pale-green seeds that five days later sprout thickly, in heaps, in her garden. Another week after that, they are almost impossible to uproot—hanging on to the soil with both hands, refusing to let it go.

Children

WE KEPT A goat one year—a kid from next door, wired to twenty feet of dog chain and clothesline cable. It had a real gift for escape. What we expected, with its mother calling for it only two hundred yards away, and her scent carrying warm and thick on the starlit night wind, I don't know. It died at the end of the cable, anchored to an elm; stiff and cold, its lips pulled back in a stupid expression. I scrambled down the hill to it, but it wasn't the goat we had known at all—just something still, and far away. There was nothing I could share with it, and anything that had connected it to our lives had vanished: it had left the earth. We were fruit-growing men, men of trees, not of animals. Its lust for the earth, and the lust of the earth itself, escaped us quickly and quietly. Without sacrifice, without a blood pact with the earth, we were not real farmers, but dreamers, hiding in fear on the far side of the world, as if the war could not reach us there—although we were the ones who had brought it, although we lived our whole lives by its rules.

The Sheep

FOR MY SISTER's sheep, we built a moveable pen out of loading pallets turned on their ends, but it was difficult to move and the ewe was quick to eat the grass inside it. In the end we led her out into the orchard every day, where she could eat the lush green grass under the trees. However, when my father weed-sprayed, she would be short of food and would bawl day and night. For that we said she was profoundly stupid. We were wrong. What we took as stupidity was the fire of a god. Gods can be as stupid as the wind, yet be full of fire and rain and the scent of powdered rock. They don't have a human intelligence. When you look into the eyes of a sheep, you are looking into the twitching of its nerves, the seasick motion of its brain as it swells and ebbs in the darkness of its eyes with every breath as it rocks back and forth in its skull. When a sheep looks out on the world through the haze of its breath it sees little light. It sees figures moving through a dark, which is not light, but the grass and the trees themselves. We were a people unused to death. We knew neither what to do with it nor how to approach it. We were without mercy. We didn't know that our lives, shadows cast up by the fires of the war, were the worship of old gods. Nor that they demanded sacrifice.

In the end, one of those weedkillers got her: 2-4-5-TP. As my father could not face death, in any form, and so could not even face compassion, or pity, as I was to do over and over I became its messenger. I dragged her out through the dust to the back corner of the farm and tried to dig a grave for her in the dry, packed earth. In that unirrigated loading ground I dug for an hour—and got down only two feet. By that time she was stiff and hard. After I'd covered her over, two of her black, shit-smeared hooves still stuck out through the snapped-off weed stalks and the sand. Furious, I shovelled more sand, to cover them, and walked away, in self-hate. That night, the dogs dug down to her and gnawed the poisoned meat off her legs. I went back every morning for a week to cover her over. After that she stunk so badly that even the dogs left her alone. Those were the thin windy skies of summer.

Siberian Elms

YEARS AFTER MY father sold the farm in haste and despair I went back to cut down the elm trees for firewood. The tree the goat had strangled itself on was one of the few that were saved. While the others towered up and clawed the birds out of the skies, it was small and runty, and let the light and air into the lawn. Today the stumps have re-grown into low brushy trees. They will not die. As my father had hoped, they are trees perfectly suited to this climate.

Yarrow

I T I S T H E dense white flower of the yarrow that sticks to me—
that flower with the scent of axle-grease and willow ash. I often picked yarrow stalks from the slope below the house and
took them into the house for my mother. I was always taking
her wild flowers, in the spring. At that point I was not to know
that her favourite flowers were freesias: succulent, grown in a
hothouse. In the years I lived away from the valley I would
sometimes wake in the middle of the night, and the stink of the
yarrow would flood the room, and I would know the earth was
real.

Slaughter

My FIRST introduction to death came from the Norwegians down the road. Every fall we would go there, and as the wind howled and snapped off the marshes, and through the sage, scattering scraps of cardboard and tumbleweeds around the yard, and stinking of snow, my father would help them hoist a huge pig on a block and tackle, and then they'd scald it, and shave it. The blood would pour into buckets, and the men's boots would be muddy with dirt and blood. They had sharp knives, and kitchen knives, all sharpened on stones, and just before it was hoisted up they would tell us to look away. The pig would be screaming—a scream that sounded like the wind. And there was snow, bright, halfway down the dark slopes of the mountain, all around, and the sky was blowing through the trees, you could see it move, and the men were so relaxed, so sure. The dogs had to be chained up, and they barked and howled. One year, one of them got away, and leapt up at the pig, and tried to drag it away. The pig looked like a man, hanging there, with terrible, stiff, hard feet, stupid feet. One year the whole damn thing fell into the mud, and the snow was cold and bitter on the air.

Windfalls

We found the cat in the late fall—Saturday, so we were home from school and down on the bottom land, picking the last of the apples—one of those oxygen-rich fall days when we were glad for the earth. There was frost in the grass, the sky was torn with cloud, and the leaves were streaming off the trees and against us. The trees were boiling like liquid methane. The grass stood in long green crystals of ice. All day the sky grew darker and darker with storm and all day a stray cat stayed with us, climbing trees, following our picking from limb to limb, quiet and patient like a bird.

Those were harsh years of falling fruit prices. The colonial society was breaking down, as it was continually breaking down, right from its inception, and the fruit industry had failed to recognize it, and innovate. Farmers had been lulled into a feeling of permanence, but permanence here is only something to reach for, not something to attain. In those days we had not discovered that and were going broke. Those were harsh years, years of growing strain in the family, as my mother grew less and less fond of farming. Her distance, her lack of engagement, was to mould us as much as the altogether different distance of my father. Those were rough years. Swaggering, my brother and I were trying so hard to be tough like our father, as we saw him, and without feeling, and so claim our time.

At dark that night, with the snow beginning to collect among the roots of the grass, we lifted the cat down out of a tree and brought her home. My mother was as shocked as we were, as we burst into the heat of the house, our faces burning with wind, and passed the cat to her. So it stayed there with us as my father went out to throw a tarp over the apples to keep them from the frost. It would have been better to let the cat stay out in the cold. Me too. For it was brought in with love and dispatched with intolerance and hate, and against that the love was too shallow, too vulnerable, in this world of darkness and winter wind that is at times all the love we have—small scraps to cling to as we struggle to understand our deaths.

But I can say nothing, for she was mine; it was while the steers stood there in the half-dark and watched her die that death got its first really good grip around my chest.

Methane

A DOLLAR WAS a whole day's wages. My brother refused the job outright—I was surprised at that. I said, sure, I would, I could do that. I did do it, but it did not bring me either praise or pride. Even the air dimmed and left me.

I took her out through the slow new snow, to the cattle pen. With the shit up to their ankles, the steers watched, silent, chewing the last, stiff stalks of their morning hay, their hot breath condensing before their faces—they were looking at the world through fog. By the time she was only the smell of wet, cold fur, I was shaking all over, and literally ran down the hill. I wanted her buried and gone, there in the marshy stink of the willows, in the frozen ground. I was desperate. The sky had blown wide open, to the height of the farthest stars above me, and at my back was a god. I did not turn around. If I had turned around, he would have been there; he would have slapped me hard in the face, with his hunting gloves, his falcon gloves. When I got back up the hill, short of breath, I stumbled into the house. The whole family stared at me, disgusted, and I felt betrayed. Stupidity, bewilderment, a frozen lack of feeling, and above them all betrayal: paying your son to kill. How can a child understand that?

That summer, when I finally got around to shoveling out that steer pen, the manure was white with mildew, and stank so heavily of ammonia that I could only dig it up for ten minutes at a time or I would lose my balance and fall down, unable to hold myself up. Yet every day the steers stood there, the insides of their heads burnt clean.

Balance

ALL WE HAD been learning, as pointless as it seemed, meant only one thing: the equation must balance, and it would balance, and it always balanced. A ripe cherry will absorb rain to neutralize its sugars, and so will split its skin, while all around it the leaves are perspiring with the heat; under certain conditions clouds precipitate into snow, just as an acid mixed with a base will produce salt. The whole world, all of it, tries to balance. The individual parts of it don't mean a thing. If you want life or nature out of it, or whatever you want out of it, then you have to protect that, and work for it and not take it for granted because it is only one of many balances, none of which means anything more to the earth than any other. The earth wants only to balance, not to be more of one thing than another.

Pruning in the Dark

ON WINTER NIGHTS after school I pruned, into the dark, under the burning stars. It was such a darkness that the trees were smoke. To catch a glimpse of the trees against the pale central bowl of the sky, I had to move all around them, dancing on the skin of sweat frozen to the horsehair liners of my gumbooted feet. But I could not focus on them. They moved just on the edge of vision, barely separate from the dark. They were the night. To see them at all, even in movement, I had to sway back and forth on my numb legs, my lungs watering with the cold. I spent my winters staring into the mouth of the sky as the colours fell out of it minute by minute, and then into the stars. They took my breath away. It was with them that I lived.

Often at that time of night when the black wood of the trees was so bitter it snapped like charcoal at my touch and the dry, musty scents of old grass rose up over my face as I brushed through it, I would find the small, greasy corpses of mice that the owls had left in the crotches of trees against the coming months of bad hunting. I never saw an owl. One did swoop down on my brother, as he walked home from parking the Cat down in the gravel pit, there where the air was flooded with the scent of willows, in the black, oily clay of the creek-bed; swooped down out of the brittle, hanging limbs of the abandoned, cankered, unpruned Moorpark apricot tree, and

brushed over his hair—dragging its claws across his scalp—
and up, silently, into the starlight: a great horned owl, with a
wingspread almost like a man's arms. Every night I would
walk the half mile through the snow back to the house and not
once did I see an owl. But the trees were mine. Only for me did
they dance. I would walk home in the dark, with the stars like
streaks of vapour overhead, and tears of wind frozen on my
cheeks. There would be no feeling left in my fingers, and I
would hold the scent of those trees with my body, the leather
of my gloves stiff as wood with that black cold.

What made those winter hours so exhilarating was the loss
of thought that came with them, the total transformation of
my mind into the trees and clippers and grass and snow and
stars. I was the air, the mountains on the flanks of the valley,
the thin light overhead, the northern lights flaring up over
Daly Ridge. My thoughts were trees and snow and air. I was
alive.

The Taste of Time

IT WAS ROMANCE to think we could preserve our life on the land, actually protect it like a game reserve, keep it wild. Our economy was not our own: the world had changed, and our wildness with it. We sold our fruit to the world; in return, we received money, which we used to buy man-made objects from the world. We filled up our lives with things and removed ourselves from the earth, where things did not exist, but had a larger, more spiritual dimension. But we did not know that then. We still had a few years left. I continued to prune, my brother continued to drive the tractors into the ground and into the trees, and my father continued, with increasing desperation, to finance the dream. And just as we were cut off from the world of time—that grey sky above us, pressing in on us—so were our lives insular: my father was the manager, my brother was the driver, I did the farming, and we lived together in mistrust, bound closely to the farm, but to each other only through that. Simply, my father, who had come from Germany to farm and to be free, could not stand farming. He needed the earth, but farming left too much bile in his mouth. The desperation of it—and the culture of it—drove him to hate himself and fed his hatred of people and the world.

The impulse to flee Germany was no different from the farming experience that left nothing but debt and incomprehension in my father's hands. He had no time for the yellow leaves that sank cold and wet off his fall trees and clung trembling to the grass until one night their light vanished and in the morning they were leaves of the earth. Already he was moving too quickly. But it is only in the aftershock of watching the leaves fall that time comes, the taste of time—like rain suddenly beating with its tiny dulcimer hammers on the aluminum roof of the shed, like one of the ancient gods gone mad as an AM radio in the mountain night, catching static and music from two thousand miles away in the Texas desert. On the other hand, I had all the time in the world to stare at leaves and to taste them. They are bitter. They are bitter like the stains of nightshade and red osier dogwoods along slow-moving creeks. They are bitter like old twigs snapping underfoot, hollow. They are bitter like the first scent of fall. But that's all I had.

Night Reception

WITH THE LIGHT of the leaves suddenly flaring like the sun out in the cold, and burning right through the rain, in the shade of the elms our house was small and dark. The light seemed to come out of the sky itself; and through the loose, torn fabric of that sky, hanging shredded over the valley, the wind poured, from Siberia. Those nights as the mice scuttled and squealed in the walls I huddled in the concrete basement, listening, through the old shortwave antenna, fifty feet of cable running along the peak of the roof, and from there the fifty feet to one of the elms, through those wires and those nails, and that tree, especially, to Houston, Sacramento, Spokane, Seattle, Vancouver, San Francisco, San Diego, Portland, and Dallas. Sometimes I listened to all of them at once—shrill, whining with the background noise of stars. Their signals fluttered as the tree swayed and bucked in the wind. They swept over me like the sea—the sea I had never seen. The next morning the trees would be burning themselves—grey fire. These were not the leaves burning, but the *trees*. They were fires of the earth, older than men. They were women, who knew the cold, intimately. They were flowers of stone. The air between them was quiet and sure of its place—something you felt with your whole body, all at once. It took me thirty long years to realize this once and for all. Slow work. The trees have never forgotten it.

Jackpine

EVERY FALL IN the first drifting owl-feather flakes of snow my
father and Otto would leave on a Friday morning before dawn
and drive west above Princeton, up onto the high jackpine
slopes: weeds, thrashing up as thick as grain out of an old
burn. For two days there, they would fell trees. Late on Saturday, as the stars flashed like birds through the bare branches
of the apple trees around the house, they would return, the old
green International creaking under a ten-foot high, sweet-
smelling load of poles. With these poles we staked the young
trees. Rough-barked and sticky with pitch, they brought the
wilderness close. Even more important were the stories my father brought back with them: stories of drifting snow and
whiskey jacks swooping down out of the trees to steal food, of
crows laughing, unseen, among the branches, and of the quiet,
echoing cathedral of the forest, cut only by the steady swish of
the swede-saws and the "thock thock" of the axes. After years
of being carried away by these stories, one Sunday afternoon
we all piled into the car and drove the hour and a half west
onto those high slopes. When we stopped the car it was at a
dirty, scrubby forest of oppressive grey light. I walked in for
three minutes, listening desperately for crows and jays, but
there was only a dull creaking swoop of wind and the swish of
a car cruising past on the road. Before I could walk in farther,
into the forest of my imagination, until I was completely alone

and within the stories, my father called us back. We drove home without a word, and without stopping. Something that had been there, that was real and palpable, the ancient, sacred forest, had vanished, and it scared him, and with that fear his heart raced, and he drove fast. In the back seat, I was wild and confused.

Sunday Driving

TWO HUNDRED MILES north to Kamloops, two hundred miles down through the Fraser Canyon to Hope, and one hundred and twenty-five miles over Allison Pass, to home, without a stop, at seventy miles per hour: the ritual of a Sunday Drive. An alternate route: two hundred miles south to Grand Coulee Dam; home by mid-afternoon. At Grand Coulee we would ride the elevators down into the dam and look over the catwalk at the huge turbines, gleaming in their vast polished concrete cathedral. All around us and behind us, the concrete throbbed with the taut tension of the river. And we believed it. We believed that by driving so fast we had driven past ourselves and had arrived at the heart of power. The only tool my father had was his car, and he made the best use of it he could, even though for self knowledge it was simply the wrong tool—with the black and ochre volcanic ruins of the Columbia Basin flaring up past us and then sinking down, broken only by an occasional house trailer, like the *Eagle* landing-craft on the moon, in the sagebrush, for mile on mile on mile.

When I pressed my forehead against the glass to cool my spinning head, the power poles, vertical railroad ties out among the blurred shapes of the sagebrush, lurched regularly and sickeningly past—so quickly they almost vanished altogether. The sagebrush was visible out of its shadow only for the briefest moment before it again became a grey, streaming blur. In those long streaks of smudged light, over and over and over the pale ghost of my own face, and a ghost of the angular lines of the interior of the car, with the speedometer at 70 glowing brightly, hurtled past, matching us, breath for breath.

The Test

MANY TIMES MY father drove out with me to the orchard that stretched up onto the benchland from the house, row on row on row surveyed by Major Kavanaugh in 1952, straight as beams of light. There he'd park the car under the trees, dim the lights, and talk. "We have a special gift. Even in the dark, Harold, you and I can sit here and know that these trees are unhappy—they are suffering." And then he would ask, "How can you tell?" I never answered correctly, not once. I did my best to feel the sadness of the trees in the air around us, but felt only the pressing, almost infinite weight of the darkness. I would feel a sudden and corresponding transparency surge up within myself and not find voice, but I would feel nothing to do with the happiness or the unhappiness of the trees. I thought I was missing something. I thought I was missing everything. I was wrong: we lived with each other, those trees and I, in a strange moonlit marriage of which only they knew the terms.

Primary Colours

My FATHER IS from Kuppenheim, a small village eight kilometres above the Rhine, north of Baden Baden. It was there, in the smoke, fog, and black earth, that he received his introduction to farming. Even in the 1930's the farmland there had been idle for forty years. On those abandoned and near-worthless farms, in that massively industrialized country, my father defined his life. They were small farms, a hectare or less, farmed on the weekends by men, and later women, who both lived and worked in town. It was not a valued occupation. No-one was proud to farm. The National Socialists conscripted the young children, the entire school population, to collect potato beetles in those fields, and to pick the fruit from the mossy black trees—before it fell to the grass—for the cows. It had nothing to do with money. In the thirties nobody's economy, anywhere, had anything to do with money, only with dreams —broken or unlived.

"Every time I collected a bucket of beetles I'd get points. I could use them to see a propaganda show at the theatre. And not just bugs. We'd get points for collecting scraps of iron, and cigarette wrappers, tin cans, and stuff, and for drying wild peppermint and picking up beechnuts, all sorts of stuff.

"Ya. I'd go to Franzel's house. I was ten years old. For a day's work, I'd get dinner, black bread and butter cheese. She had these cows. We'd hook up one of those three cows, they were sway-backed and cranky, hook it to a cart and stomp off like that, down the road, to her field. It was about two kilometres out. She'd set her baby down to play with the fruit in the grass, under the trees, and the sun was yellow and greasy. We scythed the grass, swathed it, and piled it on that cart. It was a slower trip home, the cart piled high with hay for the other two cows. What a stupid sort of farming.

"One day we were collecting our tools to go back to town. An American plane, a Lightning with two black pilots flashed up. So there we were. Franzel, her little baby and I dived into the grass underneath the wagon, right down in the dirt.

"So the pilots shot up the cow. A lot of cows died in that war, stupidly, but this one was hiding out as a horse!

"Ya, it should have got a medal, oh the iron cross."

Something inhuman and pitiless.

Naming

THESE THINGS ARE so much ours alone: death, slaughter, and prostitution before machines and words and law. That is our European heritage. Culture is not spawned in science, or history, or an awareness of art and the forms of human discourse, but in isolation and fear. When you are alone with the earth, things are what you name them.

Planting and Harvest

DURING THE Occupation, when my father had to crawl in the dark around the French sentries to steal whatever food he could, he was still working, off and on, for Franzel. They were planting potatoes. Franzel knew about the thefts and said nothing. At night my father would sneak those few miles back to the field, in the dark, under the old pewter-grey German stars, and steal the soft, sprouting potatoes that he had planted for her the day before. Franzel never breathed a word.

Ridicule

IN THE 1970's, when it seemed that the world would run out of oil in ten years, my father gloated, red-faced. "You watch. It won't be long now. Farmers will be the only ones with gas and equipment and chemicals. Because they produce with it. People need to eat! People won't laugh then."

Running After my Mother

IT WAS AT killing time that the neighbours first saw my parents. Directly in front of their window ran a chicken, headless, blood spurting out of its neck, then my mother, yelling, and laughing at the same time, and covered with blood, and nearly tripping, and my father, chasing her with a bloody axe.

Siberian Flats, 1972

MY FATHER WOULD shine his lights into the orchard at night at the base of Puddinhead Mountain, and blast away at the deer. Sometimes he would bring down three in a night. The lights of the truck would pick out the dark smoke of the trees, and the new buds, virginal, in the clear air, the first blossoms on the young trees, their first real spring, the air clear right up to the stars, and there would be the deer eating the trees and then there were no more deer.

The Fruit Wars

THERE WAS ONE thin, wormy, shepherd-cross of a bitch, too, and that was the worst, abandoned by two workers from Quebec, FLQ sympathisers, on the run from the RCMP.

My brother and I had been working sixty miles north that night, in Westbank, sorting and packing apples in the only storage that would rent us space. At midnight we loaded the fruit into a semi-trailer—under cover of darkness so the fruit police would not find us and confiscate the load. By that time, my father was doing his best to destroy the entire co-operative fruit-marketing system of British Columbia.

The system dated back to 1936, the result of an industry with its roots set as deep in real-estate fraud as in commerce and the possibilities of building a new country—the entire bottom of Okanagan Lake, between Summerland, Naramata, and Penticton, for instance, carved up into ten acre lots and sold, sight unseen, to prairie people—as an escape from the cold. And the land wasn't cheap: in 1909, orchard lots in Keremeos sold for $1,000 an acre at 9 percent interest, payable over three years—for orchards which themselves would not pay a return before 1919. Similarly, the irrigation systems, built hurriedly by the real estate companies, were so inadequate that in 1914 the B.C. government nearly went bankrupt paying to upgrade the systems in Oliver and Osoyoos. In short, it was an industry in which thousands of inexperienced, heavily indebted orchardists were producing fruit wholly at the mercy of their buyers. Fruit unsold within a few days would be worthless, so the growers continually bid against each other and so destroyed their prices. In the end, understandably, they begged the government to force everyone, including the independently owned packing houses into one large co-operative system. In this way they managed to safeguard their industry for another thirty years. By the sixties, however, the system had become old and stale. Many farmers were being forced out of business. With no accountability for quality and no orientation to market forces, many farmers were being forced out of business. My father wanted to get paid for his fruit, and in his despair, with all legitimate channels closed to him, he chose to do it under cover of darkness.

We started home from Westbank at 2:30 a.m. At 4:30, we ran out of gas, so we started running. At 5:30 we finally stumbled home, walked past the dog in the last convulsions of strychnine poisoning, and into the house. Dad was waiting up for us, sleepless in his guilt. He had left us at 2:30 the afternoon before. We wolfed down some bread and sausage, then went back outside to have a look at the dog, but she was dead.

Running with the Wind

ALL ABOVE US as we ran home the stars shone, and the wind was light, gritty with dust, and restless. As we ran up the road from the highway—staggering, our legs weak with fatigue—I laughed and laughed as the wind ran its body over my face and caressed my back and chest in its restlessness, like a dog glad to see me home.

7
LOVE

Supersaturation

At five years old the girls next door had a complete and detailed knowledge of sex and its implications, which I, fighting off the Lederhosen that came in regularly from Germany—stiff, uncomfortable things that rubbed your legs raw—did not gain for years. Ours was a house too heavily steeped in sex, a house riding on the crest of the wind, on a point of gravel jutting out from the orchard into the open sea.

A glass of water will only dissolve a certain quantity of salt, but if you heat the water, it will absorb far more, and will maintain it when cooled. If you suspend a string into the cooled water, salt crystals will form on it, like a shaman's spirit crystal. Our house was supersaturated like that with sex. It was nothing seen or spoken of, and I never found the string that drew the salt out of the air, out of the two-by-fours and the glass in the windows, but it was there. Occasionally I would bump into it in the middle of the night, and would taste the sweat on my lips. It was unspoken, but it was still there—like a bull who had crashed into a pen of heifers, and as he stood there for a minute in shock at his success, with the females scattering before him, he smelled their scent on the air. It was a locked bedroom door, conversations that stopped suddenly in a glow of yellow light when I stumbled into the room, complaining, sleepless. It was bad jokes that no one but a soldier in a bunker would possibly care to hear. But it wasn't in the jokes about easy women and stupid men, either, it was just there. It would burst into the room like a timber wolf caught in a snare, the rage boiling in its throat. Its name was Responsibility. Responsibility to the family name.

"You can trace our name back as far as Queen Elizabeth," my father would say in the evenings, when the homesickness came over him—thirty-three years old, echoing his father in turn. "Tell your teacher that Rommel, the Desert Fox, was your great uncle; that your great great great great great aunt married Marx. He'll be impressed, you'll see. We're not all a bunch of dumb farmers. You remember that. Marx and Rommel." So I tried to live up to that inheritance.

Lifting the Veil

I WAS FOUR years old when we moved onto our own farm. As my parents piled the wooden bushel fruit boxes of our things into the house, my brother and I walked out into the pure white sunlight and the overgrown grass. The girls next door, four and five as well, youngest of a long line of children in a bitter, disintegrating marriage, came over immediately and immediately beat us up. Once we had learned that important lesson they accepted us as friends, and until their parents' marriage finally collapsed three years later we were never separate. We spent most of our time playing house. The mysteries of their need to play that game, and the adult assurance they were able to confer upon us with it, mesmerized me.

The girls' house was a cold, unfriendly house, full of awkward silences, silent parents, and arguments that snapped closed in the other room. The one time that their mother came out and told me harshly to go home I was angry beyond belief and hurled the white-bellied alkaline stones over the bank among the sumacs, unable to comprehend why I had been shut out like that from my own life. For that is what the girls taught us: the giddy sense of taking possession of our own selves. We would walk down the muddy driveway hand in hand—a forbidden thing for a six-year-old—singing the Beatles' "I Wanna Hold Your Hand." My hand would sweat, the sky would be blowing right over us, and our freedom, our exit from the valley, our entrance into the greater, glistening world of Petula Clarke's London, "Downtown, where all the lights are bright," which we would listen to in the five-ton fruit truck, driving with Dad into town, was for a moment not just a possibility, but actually achieved. The real world did not, however, have anything to do with the orchards, and all the rest of the years of our lives in the valley were the story of these two diverging worlds within us, coming to light side by side yet unable to communicate with each other.

When I was seven, the girls moved away to Vancouver with their mother. After that, they came back every summer to spend time with their father. Every year they changed immensely: their jeans grew tighter, their clothes and hair more refined, and their interest in sex more confident, more pressing, and more confusing. Where there had been friendship, there was now supposed to be love, and where there were games played and time shared, there was now supposed to be display, and kisses, and touch. We all understood that adulthood was something we had to work hard towards, as the only exit out of the divided and powerless nature of our childhood lives. But although I worked hard at it, I was not ready to follow Patsy into her charged imagination. The one kiss she surprised me into and then broke off from laughing, when we were twelve, hurt, because I had failed: those mysteries that she had understood so well, and for so long, and which she was growing up into, deeper and deeeper, her breasts swelling, her skin softening, were closed off from me forever. I felt shut out. I wanted a friend and though love was offered to me, liberating and electric, it was also a closed door.

After that summer, the girls never returned. Their transformation into the city had become complete.

But for years that image of them suddenly standing there in the dusty driveway, mysterious and longed-for, with the familiarity of the shared intimacy of childhood, as I tore down the shale ruts from my morning sprinkler change, racing the Weimaraner, froth beading on the sides of his mouth, was a rite of passage, and longed-for the whole year, for it held within it still the possibility of us growing up into one shared and complete world.

The Greatest Show on Earth

MORE THAN anywhere else, sex showed up at the Starlight Drive-in in Penticton. Sometimes an hour would pass before the show would start, an hour spent watching the light die in the air, with the pale and tiny car lights sweeping over the huge screen, and the scent of cottonwoods coming in through the windows in a cool breeze off the lake. In our waiting we were part of the night itself.

When the MGM Lion roared I would cower behind the seats and wouldn't show my face again for fifteen minutes. I never understood the movies though: *Ben Hur, Zorba the Greek, The Bible,* a terrible film about keeping a stiff upper lip during the Mau Mau uprising, *The Devil at Four O'Clock, Hawaii.* To me they were long strings of unrelated incidents, violently alive, deeper than passionate, and whether frightening or deadly dull, more real even than that blue Volkswagen I cowered in. I was so short I couldn't see over the seats, but had to peer out between them, over the gearshift, and then out through the blades of the wipers and through the magical night that curled around us, alive. Those were the greatest movies I ever saw, because I made them up. It makes no difference that I slept through half of them, waking periodically with cold or gunfire, or crying out in icy terror at the start of the second feature when the lion roared directly into my face, with a stink of carrion and malaria and hot blood. And it was there, somewhere, between *Cat Ballou* and *Barbarella, Cool Hand Luke*, and John Wayne, that I learned finally about sex.

Giants

SEX WAS SOMETHING no one ever talked about or even mentioned, except in bluff, and in bad jokes that forced everyone into an uncomfortable intimacy. It was the children who were concerned about it all the time, hardly able to wait until they too had grown up into it and would know the secrets, and could *act* upon them. Children want to be able to act, to create with the ease and self-assurance and thoughtlessness of a god. But then everyone led such physical lives in that time that even the adults were children and thought in simple, physical terms. They were rooted in the ancient concept of a physical world which in one generation has almost entirely been lost. But that's what brought them here, to the edge, past all civilization and culture, choosing to face people by choosing to face the world instead, remaking themselves according to their conception of the physical world, leaving history completely and diving deep into time. At one time someone might have called them heroes. Or fools. Wallace Stevens would have called them giants. And that was his time, the last of it, and it is out of that we have to make our poems, out of such simple, stupid beauty.

Free Love

MY FATHER USED to kiss every woman who came to the house—on the lips: "It's an old German custom!" he'd say. They all fell for it, but their laughter was always brittle— brittle, but revealing of how much they wanted to be accepted with affection by an old and exotic world. "You can't escape it," my mother would say. "He does that to everyone." And then in the late flush of the sixties sex was suddenly free and film-makers were rushing to include as many naked women in their films as possible. I'd sit in the back seat, my face red and burning, shifting nervously, wondering why in the hell I was there, as often looking away from the screen as toward it, feigning disinterest. It was there that Jane Fonda, Ursula Andress, and Raquel Welch taught me how easy it was to un- derstand women, how trivial they were, and how helpless we were before them. What a mess.

The Baking Competition

IN THOSE YEARS before sex became a pressing problem, when the house quietly flexed above the chalky gravel and lightly fluttered in the wind as if it were only staying here on earth out of generosity and patience, Patsy and I had an unspoken agreement.

Her grandmother spent her days in bed in a two-room cabin behind their house, too weak to get up. Visiting her was easy— a few words, an old hand pressed up against the cheek, in the dim stale air, or if we were lucky, no words, no shrivelled hand against the cheek, for she'd be asleep; then a glass of milk out of the fridge, and a dried-up cookie from the tin under the sink. To see my grandmother we had to scramble down the loose gravel and cactus of the hill, over the two-by-six bridge— nailed to the tops of fenceposts three feet above the still, black water of Barcelo Creek—down the horsetail-lined road, through the mosquitoes, and through my grandfather's strange assortment of home-made machines, into her dark kitchen. Her arms would always be white with flour. Once she had given each of us a wide flowing hug, and had wiped our faces with her rancid dishcloth, we'd drink sweet home-made apple juice that tasted of windfalls and fall rain, and eat date bars, and listen to Burl Ives. Even so, she wasn't the easiest person to be around: to the very young, the old, although kind and even interesting, are frightening, protective, and strange.

That goes for my grandfather too, but then he cultivated it, nursing old socialist dreams from the twenties, old hurts and heart-attacks, that would hit him over and over from middle age.

He had huge lungs, the smile of a devil that leaked out of the side of his mouth around the black, tar-crusted lips of his pipe. His eyes literally shone, but he did have the best apples around, and to me that was a mysterious thing. I thought it was something he did with them, some light that escaped into his orchard from his house, and in my mind both the orchard and my grandfather are inseparable, but there was no secret at all: my grandfather was the only man in the country who left his apples hanging on the trees until, although worthless on the market, they reached their true, moonlit flavour.

Hard Wine

As WE DROVE into the driveway on the day we first saw my grandfather's hand-built tractor, it was stopped ten feet into the beginning of a row of trees. Behind it the grass was cut short and green. The sugary scent of the grass-sap steamed through the air and in through the open windows of the car. In front of the tractor the dandelions blew, a tall yellow forest, and hummed with bees. Through them my grandfather was walking, a canvas apple-picking bag strapped over his shoulders, picking the flower heads for wine.

My father spluttered: "He does everything the hard way!"

"The thing that really made Mom mad," said my mother many years later, "was that Dad would go out there and get stung by a bee and have *another* heart attack—and not tell anyone at all."

Strip Joint

YEARS LATER, MY brother saw one of the neighbour girls again, in Vancouver—working as a stripper in the East End. Those years of hunting and power, and of illicit danger, were not my years. I remember the years when sex was all we lived, a flavour, a personality in the air, something we moved through and which clung to nothing, but was the earth itself as it lived us all, as it moved into and through the mind and created us, and informed us with strength.

Throwing Rocks under the White Bridge

As she threw rocks into the current, I sat with my two-year-old daughter on the shore of the river, and was suddenly plunged deep into time. The river was an intricately-balanced system of levels and rapids, with no surface between it and the sky. We were sitting under the white bridge in Keremeos. Ten years ago that bridge was set alight, like a pile of tumbleweeds, by a couple of drunk kids, as a joke. We sat under the ghost of a bridge, a sagging metal Bailey bridge—without grace. Above the blue stones of the river, it is makeshift and temporary, military technology, single lane, but it is still called the white bridge. The real bridge, though, the bridge that is the light of thought that drains out of the sky both into the earth, to form the bridge, and into the mind, to form the idea of a bridge, stands in memory. It is a white heron, the colour of birch trunks against a black sky. Beneath it the river has cut itself lengthways midstream: half of it flows into a gentle backwater, while the other half dribbles down a series of mercury rapids and spills into the open air as the valley widens before it. Once the upper half of the river is out of the shadow of the bridge, it eases over the lip of the still upper pool and drains the five feet down to the lower current. When we first scrambled down the dike, the current was draining the water with such steadiness that the whole pool was moving forward, slowly, as one piece, without a tremble, without a shudder, mirroring the mountains and adding to them that black transparency that is fall water. This is the Similkameen River, river of great uplifted and counterbalanced slabs of light in perfect balance. The whole edge of this valley is a great long channel of river rock, with a few scrubs of willow and cottonwood and mint. It has a subtlety of colour, in a range of greens and browns and blue-silver, that has never been put into paint—an old idea of art, perhaps, but here still of absolute importance, as without it the river remains virtually unseen, though the highway passes beside it for sixty miles.

It was into this still pool we came to throw rocks. All along the shore the cottonwoods were yellow, streaming up into the air. The tension between that upward thrust and the stark grey stillness that is the force of a tree was at its highest, and tore. I felt it in my whole body, streaming away and yet caught, and held still: the oldest and most enduring definition of art, the ancient longing for transcendence focussed into a torch of power. Just as the Bailey bridge is the ghost of the bridge, the bridge stripped down to the idea of the bridge, it is not the living green of summer that pours continuously out into the air and is accepted by the air that has no self-definition, but the yellow of fall that brings out from trees the intense upward thrust for light.

Bait

WHEN I WAS a kid, I came to the river every February to catch whitefish. There are a lot of them in the Similkameen, but I never caught a single one. I wouldn't see them in February, only in August, their white bellies flashing with the sun as they turned, in the rapids and fast water, hugging the bottom. Every February I grubbed for helgramites under rocks in the shallow, dribbling currents. Snow and ice would still lie scattered over the flanks of the river, the sun would still set early, the wind would be bitter and cold, and the sky would be a frozen, thinned-out blue. Brown with winter-dry bunchgrass and sage-brush where they came down to and touched the valley floor, at three thousand feet the mountains would still be covered with blue snow. All the time I spent catching those twenty-legged larvae and walking from pool to pool along the dike, the wind pushing against me, slipping through the weave of my clothes and draining into me, I never caught a single whitefish. In the summers, though, I saw them, when the helgramites were dead—winged, adult shell-cases on the rocks—and the sun was overhead like a dandelion seedhead on fire.

Whitefish in a Storm

THE SIMILKAMEEN is a flat, shallow river. It is like a distillation of cold, an effluent of the sky: sharp and clear. But every spring it takes on a more human life when the sewage plant forty miles upriver flushes its settling ponds, and a long extended surf of chocolate-coloured water surges down to us. Today the rocks under the calm surface of the water are cloaked with a quarter inch of silt and algae. The bed of the river is such a uniform green-grey that the stones my daughter and I collected from the dike shone out among them like stars, or whitefish turning against the current.

We cast our rocks for five minutes. When I looked up and over the water, the mountains there, even a hundred feet from us, were swaying gently in the small waves off our pebbles, like kelp underwater or angel fish in a coral reef, slowly breathing, holding their eyes directly on us, giving a taste of rain to the air—pines in a storm off the sun.

I dug my hands into the water. When I pulled them out again they smelled of rain. We have had no rain for two and one-half months. For two and one-half months the sky has been a strip of sheet metal, burning your retinas when you touch it with your eyes, full of the harsh scents of evaporated rock, and the air has become only a gas that has evaporated off the rock.

As a kid I often stared down the same way into the puddles

of brown water that drained into the driveway from the sprinklers. There at my feet I saw clouds, miles below me, moving fast, in a high wind. I couldn't draw my eyes away, terrified that with one false step I would fall through the earth into the sky.

The Limits of Art

ALL AROUND US, day by day, the land is changing. Farming changes it, away from the earth. And because people move here to die, where property and houses are cheap, they add their porchlights to the valley floor at night, stars reflected in a muddy backwater, and domesticate the land.

Created thousands of years ago out of ritual and worship, farming is an art—its industrial face is only the metaphor of our time. In the end, it is art, not economics, which provides the parameters of the farm, art which it gave to me and which draws me back to it again and again.

On the farm, chemicals and machines are the parameters of death, the point of its greatest and most fertilizing entry into the farm. Through the farm, our art and the source of our food, they enter our lives. Chemicals and machines present a mirror picture of the farm. Like the shadow river that flows through the gravel alongside and beneath the river, in the dark, this second spirit moves through the life of the farm, pushing it out of the soil. But it is art, and it is always art, that maintains us, a wind pouring straight out of the wide throats of the cottonwoods, draining the snow from the mountains, and right through the skin on the face into the blood, the eyes clear.

Closed Worlds

MY FATHER DID not draw strength from the river. He was a man neither of this valley nor of this country. He saw the valley as a subsidiary part of a larger world, an attitude which no-one who lives here for any time shares. With the mountains floating around you like clouds, and beyond them only more mountains, and nothing of men except what you can keep in your mind, it is impossible to hold to the world. My father's connection to place was something he could abandon at will. It was not a connection to the earth. When he came up against the barrier of rock that was at the core of every man who lived here—who lived here because it was not part of the larger world, and who, as a result, could not envisage a world economy—he was powerless. Language can so easily fail us, rather than help us; there is so much it cannot touch. My father's introduction to the culture here was too slight. A nervous bravado, a brooding drunkenness, an almost surgically-removed sensitivity, a life lived through loud laughter and stories and jokes intended to deflect conversation, these are the legacy and the curse of immigrants.

Even so, it was naive of him to think he could change the people in this valley, naive to think he could rouse them from their post-colonial malaise, for it was in that mediocrity and seediness that they belonged here. As it is with people who have genuinely and with deep feeling given themselves to the earth, in that loss of self they had found something that could live for them. Unable to make himself vanish like that, for twenty years my father struggled with the social forms of this valley, trying to transform the sleepy farming practices into an industry that could survive as money became more important in life and work less so, and a farmer might suddenly be faced with an obsolete orchard and have—if he had given it no previous planning—no time in which to replant. His success was minimal. By forecasting the survival of art only through its translation into a new language of commerce he prophesied only its death. Now the art remains, but art without an economy, a language of commerce between men, is of no value in the larger world where men do use that language. You might have a place here, in the Similkameen, and enough light to live by through the work done with your own hands, but you gain as well the helplessness of the individual unsupported—and hence dominated—by stronger languages in this time. The earth must have a language with which to speak with the world, or it will have no voice.

Barbarians at the Door

THE EMPIRE IS dead now. All those countries that were in the Empire when my father came here, Kenya, Uganda, Rhodesia, Fiji, Tanganyika, Ceylon, Singapore, Burma, have gone wild. This valley and the whole vast interior of this province, have been lost in time. The money goes to Vancouver now. We are still an outpost, generating wealth and support for others—on their economic terms. That door my father closed and locked is being eaten away with snow and rust. The earth is moving in. Thirty years ago the earth, the barbarian to us in this vast country, was still at bay, and men could live here and be free. That freedom is now a chain.

Black Economies

My FATHER LEANS back in his chair, and shrugs. Swooping forward and drawing me into his breath by knotting his hands together suddenly around his glass, he begins. With this one he is on top of the world. He is the new kid on the block. Thirty years old, German, he walks into that veteran's subdivision and down the long muddy driveway, choked on the edges with weeds, to the house of Major Kavanaugh. There, over a bottle of bad whiskey, he makes such a deal for the place that Kavanaugh virtually gives him the farm.

For five years I would lease the farm. I'd pay the usual 25% lease payment, that is 25% of the crop, but that payment, and all payments, came off the cost of the property. So Kavanaugh paid for the taxes and the water, and any improvements I made. It all came off the purchase price. The lease payments were linked to the value of the crop, so this gave me a lot of room. I could rip out half the orchard and replant it, and send the bill to Kavanaugh. For my own time! To plant an orchard for nothing!

From this enviable position he took on the glow of a god, just as the blond, tall, American soldiers of his youth were his gods, as they clanked and clattered into Germany, casting such a spell over him that he eventually followed them to the New World. All those years of propaganda that Germany would rule the world—which blew over Germany from the

year he was born—gave him an easy sense of ownership, and
could bring him to the new world without humility. It was
such a strong force that it could even drop him among the soldiers that fought his people, in a country that had bombed Europe to rubble and was then able to force its economic power
upon it. And they did try to push humility on him: for five
years hardly a man in the valley spoke to him. One old man
who lived a half-mile down the road, in a small cabin on an orchard of sand and gravel that always seemed in its neglect to
be no more than a few days from death, used to stop us on the
road and mutter at us. His eyes were a bird's eyes, with no
mind behind them, only air. He used to send letters to my father, unsigned: "Your sons will not come home from school."
The common thing was just to call my father a fucking German; so this man's hatred was something special: distilled, and
pure. And eventually such men broke him, and spat him out.

Broken English

THIS SUMMER I heard my father speak German for the first time in twenty years. In German he is cultured and measured, but in English he is rough and hasty, bad-tempered, without subtlety and at times without either tenderness or understanding. English is an attitude—a language and a way of life learned, by imitation, on the farm, and suited only to the world of work and talk during work on the farm.

Drunk Driving

My FATHER WAS the new kid on the block. Across the road from him in that Veterans' Land Development—the old Barcelo Ranch of sagebrush and prickly pear cut up into twelve acre orchards in 1952—was Walter's lot. Walter would spend his days driving his short-box Dodge pickup, his back as straight as a sheet of plywood, staring straight ahead, with his dog, a silver ghost-like Weimaraner, at his side. The truck was a pale blue, faded by the sun and whitened by the calcium of the farmyard sprinklers. When you ran your hand along the fenders it left a white film, like powdered salt. Just like Walter, Walter's dog was a creature of legend. Taunted by the neighbour's son, he'd turned to bitterness and madness, and lunged for everyone who came near. With Walter, in that truck though, he was calm, and filled with importance. The two of them spent their days driving around Cawston, at 10 m.p.h., a bottle of Jack Daniels in a crumpled brown paper bag between them. Whenever they met the highway that scurries briefly through our valley before climbing down into the Okanagan at Osoyoos, and then up Anarchist Mountain and east to Canada itself, they would stop.

Canada! While Walter was driving away his life, I was in school just a block away. And there, in those chalky rooms that smelled of sweat and oil, heat and urine, we were taught that we were Canadians. Since we were children, we believed it. But this is the Interior. Canada is the Toronto Dominion Bank building that used to stand at the corner of Broad and Yates in Victoria, tall, stark, gritty, and cold. Yet Canada does exist. The highway will take you there. And every time Walter stopped at the highway, he stared straight ahead. His gaze was thin and pinched. This was the dog's moment in the sun. Sitting there beside Walter, he'd very slowly pivot his head. For a minute he'd stare out through his amber eyes to the right, then just as slowly he'd turn his head again and just as mistily stare down the road to the cascade of ocean light in the gap in the valley to the west. Then, with the same intense, measured slowness, he'd swing his head back and stare straight ahead. That was Walter's cue, and the truck would once again roll slowly forward, across the highway, and up into the orchard land that lay along the dusty, magpie-flecked flank of the mountain, above the valley. But you couldn't watch. You couldn't watch him drive the mile from the highway to his orchard. It took too long. Your mind would stall out. Even if you said, "I'm going to look straight at that truck until it fades away in the distance," you couldn't do it. You'd find yourself turning away.

Chickens

EVERY MAN gets his share of luck to use up as he needs it or sees fit. My father's came in one big load, one sudden blaze of headlights ahead of him on an icy winter road, and he used it up all at once. It lasted him for only a dozen years. By the time he was forty, he was trapped inside his life, replaying it, adding to it, embellishing it, for he had been stripped of his dreams—had replaced action with memory. But that is to go forward in time. Standing back there in 1963, my father worked with his hands, like a man possessed, to run twenty-five acres of orchard without a hired hand. Across the road, Walter suddenly realized that he need never again in his life think. It was a tremendous relief. Hardly skipping a breath, he knew all he needed was to mimic my father: if my father went out to spray lime-sulphur, Walter would be out two hours later with a great yellow fan bursting out of his sprayer. Ashen-faced, he would sit on the seat of the tractor in front of it, chewing on the end of a cigarette, squeezing the juice out of it between his teeth. If my father went out to spread fertilizer, the thin odor of ammonia burning out of it, searing the deep cracks in his hands, Walter would be out there two hours later with his tractor and his trailer heaped high with water-stained paper sacks. There, with his bucket and his tobacco can, as the light sank fitfully out of the air, he would pace in slow circles under the black snags of his trees, spreading the white pellets. From a distance he looked like a man feeding chickens, gently clucking to them softly and stupidly under his tongue.

Discing the Snow

ONE COLD JANUARY day in the chalky shadow of the full moon that was like a sheet of ice held up in the air, the weather drove in from the north, as it does in great slow cycles with every full moon. A frozen skin of breath lay over the entire earth. All the oxygen had congealed and fallen out of the air. The air was almost pure nitrogen, and sharp, and cold. Even at noon the sun cast long snakelike shadows between the trees, weaving them together, spilling them across the road and into the matted grass and drifts at Walter's. That January day, my father looked restlessly out of the windows as they surged in their frames from the force of the wind, and then laughed and suddenly blurted out to my mother that he was going out to have a little fun.

Outside, his cap pulled low over his ears, he hitched up the disc-harrow to the tractor, looped the harrow behind it with a frozen length of chain, and went out to cultivate the snow, the headlights flaring ahead of him into the storm, the trees blazing in the light. Behind him the disc sliced through the drifts and turned them over. Behind it, the harrow raked them smooth and loose again, so they would no longer hold a man's weight.

The wind tore that snow off the ground in a big white cloud, like a storm of dust on the prairies in 1934, hurled it into the driveway and packed it down as hard as cement. That was at 3 p.m. Two hours later when it was already dark, the tractor was in the shed again. And then all of us—my father, with a cup of coffee easing through his veins, my brother and I stumbling in our nylon snow suits, and my mother shivering in her loose-woven Indian sweater—broke our way down the driveway. With each step my father snapped through the crust of snow and jarred his teeth. My mother came behind, thin-boned and shivering, her voice as thin and cracked as a sparrow's, stepping in each deep well left by his feet ahead of her. My brother and I came up at their sides, running on top of the snow. The sky was indigo, a thought burning at the back of the brain, in the eternal night. The trees rose up at our sides in black, haunted thickets. The moon burned on the drifts.

In that light we walked out to Walter's. Beneath us and stretching out around us under the trees, flat and without shadow, the snow took on more and more of the light from the air. By the time we reached the edge of the orchard, it was glowing around us with a cool white fire, while the sky no longer gave any light at all. There, across the road from Walter's, we crouched behind the black trunks of the trees, the thin, weedy grass at their trunks rustling and shaking itself free of snow as we stepped into it.

In the clear air that night you could have seen him from a hundred miles away, the one unbroken headlight of his tractor lighting up the branches of his trees and casting long, rapidly moving shadows before him. He was discing his snow in the dark. As if this were the miracle of a saint or the sudden and unexpected incarnation of a god in an age of doubt, we watched. We watched for ten minutes, and then my mother said she was cold, so we retraced our steps, like birds, back to the house. In that half hour, we were all born. As little as it was, that was the energy that carried my father for the next six years, that lived in him and burned until it was only a small heap of ash in his gut. As we turned to walk in, a car passed us on the road, lighting up a great fan of air all around itself, its wipers fighting to push aside the fine, needle-sharp crystals of

snow on the wind. To look at the sky was to look at the base of
a black mountain, above which there were no stars. It was that
moment in winter, some years only a day, some years an entire
month, when the earth is completely the earth, when there is
nothing beyond us.

Past and Present Time

TONIGHT THE moon is pale behind the black charcoal of the trees. The river is frozen and the wind tears at my face, rising right out of the stones. The river and the mountain pick up the light of the moon the way water collects in a basin like distilled air. The moon is why I live here. The moon and the stars. They fill the sky. And through the stars I can possess what is lost or nearly forbidden to us here—the past. It is not ours: my father renounced it when he came to this country. It is something that I make, myself, out of stars and fitful reading, and a need for speech.

Two things are certain: time can be recaptured in its entirety and old ways of earth can be reclaimed or lived by touching earth. And although one may be adrift from men by living in this valley—a kilometre down in this scarred, almost tree-less mountain trough of sagebrush and bunchgrass and crumbling cliffs, an old lake bed from the melting of the last glaciers, where the sky is the earth, and trees, and snow—men come here, and so change us. We might export to the rest of the country, and to the world, fruit and lumber and gold, but our thoughts remain with us: they are from a world too far removed. Since we live with the earth, we live in the past, or an extension of the past into the present that society cannot recognize because it is not part of society. It is deeply personal, and physical.

Getting the Real Work Done

WHEN WE WERE still a part of the Empire, natives made up the large crews that were needed for pruning, thinning, and picking the fruit and vegetables. In the thirties and forties, the work was done by Doukhobors, as their communal villages in the Kootenays collapsed. In the fifties, it was the Germans and the Dutch—all violently disliked because they would work cheap, and they would work hard. By the mid-sixties the farmworkers were the young fleeing the cities. They came with long hair, long, flowery cotton dresses, LSD, a politics alternately sloppy and brilliant, on the run from Vietnam, and with names like Butterfly Sunshine, and with children named Blueberry and Blossom. In five years, with all their sex and their idealism, they were gone as well.

They came into our lives briefly and changed us forever. They lined up, for two hundred yards at the Kaleden intersection, with their sleeping bags and guitar cases, travelling through. They gave us a non-industrial vision of the earth. My father would stay up late with them, drinking, in the red and white tiled kitchen. In exchange for their politics, he would teach them *Skat*. "I learned it on the ship from Hamburg. A two week *Skat* game. It never stopped." It is the perfect game for late nights. As full of chance as any other, it carries, however, the myth that the skilled player will win, no matter how bad his cards. The result is shouting, beer bottles smashed down on the table, and roars of laughter, all night.

After them, came the Québecois, fleeing from RCMP persecution over their violent ambitions of freedom in Quebec, and from a stagnant economy and crippling unemployment. They were followed in the late seventies and the eighties by university students from Montreal, out to earn money for their studies in the fall. Today even they are dwindling and labour is increasingly hard to find.

The French years were years of promise and cultural growth, but also years of occasional and random violence. A few Québecois in Osoyoos were beaten with a pipe by local teens, a few were beaten in their tent on the dike in Keremeos, the headless body of a French girl was found in a greenhouse in Cawston. For five years there were no benches on Main Street Keremeos; the workmen took them down to keep the French on the move: "They are not clean. They discourage tourists. They buy nothing."

For a few summers, though, the valley was almost a part of Quebec. From those years we learned that men and women could move through the trees with gentleness and humour.

Now there is no one to work the farms.

Baptism

No one who has dipped into the silk water of the Similkameen River in the summer can ever leave this valley unchanged. For miles the river stretches wild along the edge of the valley. In the bush lining the riverbanks you will come again and again on teepees and shacks of driftwood, old fire pits, where the French Canadians have set up camp. To surface from the water as the light slams into your face is to see, for an instant so short you may not notice you have seen it, into the eyes of a god of feathers and bark and smoke. In the late seventies, whole miles of the river were taken over by the French who camped there, nude, amidst the cottonwoods and willows. They would put on clothes only if they had to go into town for work. They burnt away in the sun, like leaves. When I wrote a letter to the editor of the local paper asking him to apologize for insulting the Québecois—my co-workers, my teachers, and the only tourists we were ever going to get—he rebuked me by calling me a self-confessed transient, and so of no account.

8
DEPARTURES

Lizards

IN FALL, ONCE the trees have dropped their leaves and stand naked in the light, blind and no longer drinking the air, we would begin the pruning that would carry us through to April, when the flowers were pushing out of the twigs—cold, sexual fires. The trees are women, girls, creatures of the air—stone-scaled lizards, as feather-thin as birds.

Leavetaking

TIME BURNS. The blue sky evaporates away; the air is wet and cold. The sky is thick, clotted, and drowning with cloud. It has been months now since the swallows gathered in clouds like grasshoppers, their chests flashing the green of water beetles, their backs as purple as dusk water rolling away—a great heave and shudder in the air, huge bees, leaves scattering before the wind. Then the starlings rose sudden as a cough out of the stony fields of alfalfa, drifting and settling and rising again, the black seeds of pigweed. Now it is the beginning of pruning. All fall the air has grown more and more empty of life. In late September, the crows gathered to leave, weighting down the branches of the poplars like old, tattered, whalebone corsets. The geese left, and the sandhill cranes from the Mackenzie Delta, slipping south, day after day, high, until we passed through October and suddenly realized they were no longer there. With each successive departure I have felt more and more cut off—more and more alone with an increasingly hostile earth.

The fire has drained suddenly and unexpectedly out of the soil. The air is filled with a great foreboding. Now the robins are gone and the valley is left to the hawks, snatching cats out of the tall grass, and the magpies, shimmering blue and white and black through the rabbitbush and speargrass, the birds of death. The sky is pale, drained of colour. There appears to be no living thing. Then we vanish into the world and lose track of the days.

It is in this season, when the earth is more familiar than we had thought we could bear, when the earth is almost ready to open out into speech, that we begin to cut at the trees, to open them to the light, so that in the summer, when they are thick and hot with leaves, we can move among them and through them, like pale flies.

Waiting for the Women

A FEW LEAVES would clatter around my feet. The wind would be out of the north, bitter, stinging my face. As I moved among the trees the branches would fall around me with soft thuds into the damp earth. I would slip and slide on the wind-fall apples, slug-white and sweet-smelling, that lay hidden in the grass like salmon thrown out on the shores of creeks choking with yellow leaves. Month by month I would burn off the old year in this activity until I vanished into rain and snow and cold. Those were the short days, the days of darkness, days of rising in the dark and trudging home in the dark under stars, eight hours later, and in that day, two or three hours of sun, breaking out of the shadows of the mountains to reach us here, almost under the earth. The sun might have been hardly there, but all night the moon was present, steady and cold and clear, a drink of ice water.

In the spring, when the last of the snow had drained into the soil, when the sun was made of water and the air was warm as the skin of a woman's back, lying out in the grass, the robins would return. Suddenly one day they would be there—the males, perched in the trees, dazed, ruffled. The females would follow two weeks later. In that two-week lull, the males would claim their territories and gorge themselves on the apples, brown and pulpy, that lay under the trees. All winter the apples would be white-fleshed, red-skinned, perfectly preserved under the snow, but as soon as they thawed in the new yellow sunlight the rot would begin. Within two days they would be soft and brown. Within a week they would be bubbling and fermenting in the low spring sun. The robins would become so drunk on this first fruit that they wouldn't be able to fly. They'd stagger from sleep to sleep and grow fat and slow in the open air under the stars. Then the females would flare back and it would be spring, and the light would look like it was pressed out of sap.

A Pruning Lesson

It was blossom-time, 1970. The flowers were white on the limbs—the bees filling the air, heavy and fast and angry with work, the scent of the blossoms so thick that it poured continually into me, all afternoon. In the end there wasn't room for a single thought: I was living inside a flower, inside a tree's tenderness. As the bees swarmed over and around me to drink the nectar out of the flowers—yellow condensations of the sun, droplets of amber that had risen out of the sea of the night, so full with the energy of night that they were burning up in one long, high whine—I struggled to make sense of the trees.

Pruning is taught as half art and half science—science interpreted through art. You can manage it out of the art alone, but since art is so much less a repository for memory than science, you must learn the art on your own, from the air—you have to invent it. Pruning is a religion, a secret knowledge passed from father to son. That day in 1970, my father gave me ten minutes of instruction, regimented and simplistic. With that I had to prune those trees. It was useless. So I had to learn it from the air. Before I'd cut a limb, or even a twig, I'd pace around for five minutes in confusion and fear. After a single cut I'd pace around the tree again and look through it again at the air. It was torture. The sun poured over the whole orchard and collected in the cupped arms of the tree. All around, the trunks were bright, humming with heat and sap, and the dandelions blew around my feet, on fire. Row on row on row surrounding me, the trees were bursting into slow flame. And farther, in the depths of the air, in the trees and brush skirting the orchard, the meadowlarks hollered at each other, the males, staking out their ground. So I listened to them, and sang back, and they answered.

Cold-Blooded

OVER THE YEARS, the work grew more and more familiar. These days I drift among the trees as I prune, cold or hot as the day is cold or hot, like a snake, or a fish, indistinct from water, or work, or air.

Half a Life

SIX MONTHS OF every year, half a life, is spent pruning. It is the unacknowledged creative work of the farm. Most men hate it. The women know nothing of it. To them it is one more day, and then one more again, in the tension that is built up in this life between women and men. In the early sixties that tension broke. Most of the German women in Osoyoos died; women who had come over with their husbands from Silesia in the spring of 1929—and among them my mother's parents, Bruno and Martha Leipe. Young, idealistic labourers from the crowded cities of the East, they dreamt of setting up an agricultural and cultural commune in the Okanagan Valley. Behind them was a country where Communists and National Socialists held huge private armies of millions of men and used them on the streets against each other. They came here to rebuild the colonial dream that was dropped by the English fifteen years earlier when war fell over Europe—claiming with their bodies what the war had failed to gain. When they arrived in this wild country, however, they quickly realized that land was so plentiful and cheap that there was no division of men according to class—hard work could achieve more for a single man than could collective work against all the history of old Europe. They no longer had any use or need for a commune. One by one they bought orchards in Penticton, Oliver and Osoyoos and nearly all of them lost their wives: in the early sixties their women all contracted a pesticide-induced cancer of the cervix and died—in the space of three or four short years.

Suddenly the men were left with nothing and they shrivelled up, alone with their trees and the wind and the sun.

A Man of '29: Hans Feldt

1977. (5 A.M. LATE JULY). The light is just rising out of the grass to fill the air. He lurches like a bear out of the black shadow of a cherry tree, waves, and stumbles, slowly, down the road—unshaven. For three months he has been living as a guest of the government in the old Haven Hill retirement home, the old hospital looking out over Penticton.

His house was unpainted shiplap, flooded with the musty, shitty, rotten stink of rats—they had even nested among his old clothes. Books and magazines were scattered over the floor, their pages warped with rain; a few broken cups, a painted, ceramic beerstein, a few postcards from vacations in Russia before the War, before the Revolution, before all of us, when Russia was still part of Europe, and bourgeois. And junk: sheets that had been unwashed for years, on a bed that had lost its springs twenty years before; books and photographs; spray calendars; two boxes of thin books—his own. The first was a dream: *Capitalism is Not Free Enterprise*. The second was a revision: *There is No Santa Claus*. He used to walk the eleven miles to Penticton, right along the centre line of Naramata Road, with the cars surging past him out of the blind corners like gunfire, to give away his books on the street; wearing sagging pants, a length of sisal twine for a belt, a white shirt gone black with dirt over the years, and a greasy wool overcoat he had worn since the beginning of the Second World War, when he lost touch wih his family in Magdeburg.

He had become a night lake that you walk into in August, but neither see nor feel on your skin—it is as thin as the air, a caught wind. What was feminine or civilized in his life was dead. Without women banally going through the forms of civilized life, as the last Romans did in the Middle Ages, painfully copying out the ancient books by hand, there is no civilization here: no greetings exchanged, no good silver, no church bargain basements, no Red Cross blood drives—essentials. Without his wife's care the grape trellis along the house fell down and the grapes grew wild and unpicked, a huge tapestry in the bunchgrass, trailing down through the broken bottles and broken ladders of the hill, and the sky like something caught at the back of the throat. All his kitchen garbage, the entire record of his life, he simply heaved over that slope, right off the front step of the house. He never bought a fridge, kept his woodstove, never cleaned it, and sank into politics, and, like so many self-taught men, did so in anger, rage and pain. His orchard, like an extension of his mind, on that steep clay cliff above the lake, was planted without rows—the tangled order of a fairy tale, where the characters all change places over and over, and are all bound in a knot at the end, like the morning light of the sun. They burn in the mind, and burn the mind away, leaving room only for the world. It was a dangerous place to work. In half a second a man could slip and drive the tractor off the edge of the cliff, three hundred feet down through the bluebirds and hummingbirds to the lake.

It was to this madness that Hans Feldt had escaped that night. It was a lonely journey for him, each step taking him farther into a hopeless past. But in the rhythms of the earth it was important that the two of us meet. On those white clay cliffs, high above Okanagan lake, he had haunted me for the entire summer, while I fought hard to find my way back to the land. My entire life had taught me to renounce the land as a form of death and when I found it in any living form to make it into a form of death. Now I was trying to transform it, or re-see it, as a life-giving power. And there I lived his life. I'd be

above the lake, atop a swaying, shaky ladder forty years old
and as light as balsa wood with sun, thinning the apricots, in
the red trees. The slope was so steep that if I looked out I
could see only sky, and below the sky, directly in front of me,
three hundred feet down, but so close I could touch it, the lake
like a voice.

So used to drifting away from me in the rhythms of work,
my mind had entered the rhythms of the old, old dreams Hans
Feldt had poured into the land. I was working there in a swel
tering heat, ten or twelve hours a day, dressed in a pair of cut-
off jeans, and runners, in the air—the voice of time. In the evenings I'd sit on the edge of the orchard and watch the sun
flare, ancient, above this European farm. This was not Canada. It was the earthly paradise, a synthesis of Italy, Provence
and Lake Constance, and childhood, the lost kingdom of
childhood, which is pure perception—a helpless, unfocussed
feeling of age and loss, immeasurably old. That was the year I
read Virgil under a pear tree by my porch light, the grass
around me burning with crickets, the air clear, the mosquitoes
driven off by the wind. I read the *Aeneid* as if it were the world,
as Virgil himself might have read it as he put each word down
after carving it out with his tongue. And then, with the words
swimming within me, trying to reform themselves inside me
into their original life, shocked and awake, I would walk out of
the rim of the light into the total and sudden dark, thick with
stars, and the deep, deep, unexpected wells of time.

That was the year my grandmother gave me as a keepsake
my grandfather's recording of the *Pastorale*. The conductor
was Bruno Walter, the romantic. The jacket had a picture of
draught-horses, heavy and industrial, plowing. As the mosquitoes rose out of the grass, I played the record over and over:
the sky opened into the blackness of the stars, and dead-tired I
would collapse into my dusty, un-made bed, unable to sleep.

That morning meeting under the cherry tree was necessary.
It was a glass of dark wine passed between Hans Feldt and
me, sipped from and then cast into the ground.

It was a living wind that poured through the trees that summer. It taught me that the greatest mistake we can make is to believe in history: everything changes, what we bring to the passage of time is ourselves. What we see when we actually touch the earth, in those places and moments when others have touched the earth before us in that space, is all the world: there is no progression or progressive civilization of man and earth through time.

That summer in Naramata I lived with the goddesses of ancient Greece, and with the hard-working immigrants of the thirties, lost in their poverty and dreams of an ancient peasantry. The star-studded sky above me, a sky as black as Minoan lacquer ware, was Greek. It was the colour of the mind: not what a blind man sees, but what a man with sight can see when he goes blind with sight.

One afternoon a contractor brought three dump-trucks to haul Hans Feldt's house away. At the first touch of the bulldozer blade the house exploded in a cloud of bats. The men shut their machinery down to an idle, and with the exhausts of trucks, loader and a D4 pouring out a nearly transparent heat-ripple, for five minutes the bats fled out of the house in a great fearful rustle into the hot desert air.

I forgot to breathe.

9
FAITHS AND RELIGIONS

Drops of Rain

A GATHERING ONCE walked in a long procession the three thousand feet to the top of K-Mountain above Keremeos to wait for U.F.O.'s. We have a plethora of right-wing Christian cults, Roman Catholics, Anglicans, Baptists, a Calvinist/Buddhist, and all the other imports of civilization, but the strongest holiness, and the strength in which they root themselves, is the primitive gods that in this late time live directly within the world, which is in the mind within objects. That is the legacy of language. If you pick up a stone in this valley, it is a small piece of voice, a droplet of the sky.

Space

MEN AND WOMEN came here in the time of two great, destructive wars that destroyed all meaning in civilization—including the Church. It is as if a brush fire had raged through the whole valley, burning everything clean and leaving a uniform blackness that caught up the wind and stained the air. That is our night, charcoal scattered over the light. Everything had to be rebuilt—and they came to build a future and to redefine—and so to purify—the past. And we are the future but so transformed through the lens of the land that to them we are unrecognizable. We are a new language—of stone and water and air. So life achieves a balance: just as my invisible mother became the physical world around me, all of Europe can be found here, in this valley, piece by piece, Marx with Homer, Hegel with Dante and Mozart. Its only unity is that it is all here together, at one time, in the land, and giving us the name of the land. It is time that does not exist.

The Living Gods

In the end the dreams and the bone-weary work do not count. That crushing of desire through work that has been part of us since the priestesses of Demeter invented agriculture, is not the centre of the world. It didn't supplant the old gods of forest and air, but while the dream-kings were out hunting in the mountains and forests, outside of society, the women were home, secure in their place *within* society. With the ritual domestication of animals and grasses came the gentle light of woman, the smell of earth in a woman's skin that had not before entered the air. Even today, these are the living gods, for in the living mind any strength that enters the body and the mind is the strength of a god: the erect phallus, the fire in wine, the power in the legs of a goat as it leaps over the rocks, the silver plunge of a river, the slow green flame in the germ of wheat, the moon dragging the tides across the ocean and through our wind-swept bodies, the surf. We think as much by completed conception as we do by thought. Like all modes of focussed union, it is a language. It can be understood only in its own words, the thoughts it alone can generate out of the blank pool of the mind. In both women and earth a seed takes root and comes forth living, with a god in it. To channel this power into agriculture, however, as a new worship of the old earth, caused the hunters to hunt the fields, towns, and women of their new civilised life, as they had hunted in the past the boars on the slopes of Mount Ida and hammered out gold masks for their dead, in recognition of the sun—heavy, gleaming purifications of the earth. Light is the ultimate heaviness.

Some women prefer this aggression and this closeness. Physical life and physical thought had more importance in the past, for they were actively acknowledged and developed, and not left simply to haunt us. If you take on the role of a god or worship a god, you create that god, out of the blank matter of the earth. The energy is within us all. It must be directed, and it must be directed at a point outside of us. The human mind is a receptacle and when so channelled into a specific direction is capable of wonders, and death. So it was that men and women traded their respective powers in society, and men took on the roles of women. Economics, money, business—these are not the life of men, but of women, with their passion for order, but if economics, money and business are not the life of men, men can still enter them and manipulate them to their own ends, for great profit. They can do it, and they do do it, but there is a price: in return they must drink, and must allow the god within the wine to tear them to shreds.

Sauerkraut

SURE ENOUGH, as soon as my father reached the height of his career, he suffered great misfortune: thirty acres of cabbages plowed under because the marketing board returned him three cents a pound—less than the cost of picking them; twenty-five acres of tomatoes, the plants bought cheap—and a dry yellow, and losing their leaves—from Michigan, that began to ripen on the 28th of August, and which were frozen dead that night in the rocky field at Siberian Flats, a freakish wind coming straight off the mountains, draining through the high meadows of lupins and larch and peat, out of the tundra of the stars; seventy-five acres of onions droughted when the power line over the old Fairview mine site was wiped out for ten days by fire and all attempts to get a diesel pump working to draw water from between the fins of the trout in Keremeos Creek, in flood, failed.

When the cabbages were plowed under they rotted in the black, stony earth. They became brown balls of mucus, and rose in a sulphurous gas. It sat heavy over the ground for months. One old man, living there in one of the last houses of the old, waterless townsite of Upper Keremeos, claimed that as long as those cabbages were rotting in the ground his rheumatism was cured and he could move his arms at will. Great flocks of vultures came up from the marshes of the Indian reserves at Similkameen and Chopaka to feast on those fermented fields.

The last shipment of cabbages went to supply the Polish fishing fleet off the West Coast. Late one night a call came in from the sea, full of the static of storm: the cabbages were rotten and were exploding in the hold. "Do not," my father said years later, pounding the table, bitter, "store cabbages with cherries. Don't let the packing house do it."

Half an Acre of Cabbages
a Night

IT WAS POINTLESS to sit around trying to shoot the marmots. That was obvious. Some lesser man might have given up, but at 4 a.m., when the starlight was just beginning to thin the air, my father set one stick of dynamite down each of their sandy runs, there among the stumps of the first pear trees planted in the Okanagan carried by packhorse from Oregon in 1898, and blew them all to hell.

Watching the Mountains Breathe

OVER AND OVER my father was being taught a lesson, but he
did not realize it until it was too late and he had lost even the
land he loved. Years later, when I had finally given up on
farming myself, and had buried for the winter the last of my
ten thousand nursery trees in sawdust and the late November
soil, I was standing there at Brushy Bottom, soaked from the
water I had just poured over the trees to keep out the frost. My
knuckles were bleeding from draining the pump in the dark
and cold, for water-soaked skin cuts as easily as a leaf. The
night rose ancient above me, and as I stood there a great
weight seemed to rise off the mountains. For the first time in
years they breathed openly. A god had left me—a vicious, vin-
dictive god. I had come again into the earth. For the first time
in years I broke out laughing; and chill, and rich in my cold,
walked as dark as starlight up through the mud and the mock-
orange and the tangled hulks of the elderberries to my truck
and home, in the wind and gravel. If you had been standing
beneath one of the pines there you would have felt the first
snow drifting in on the wind, but you would not have seen me
there, only the darkness.

The Packinghouse Directors
Make Their Way Home

IN THOSE YEARS men drank in earnest. It was an obligation, a serious business, and a rite. One night in 1969 my father and his friends were driving Ramsay home in his brand-new Buick. It was 2 a.m. They were on their way back from a directors' meeting at the co-op packinghouse and Ramsay was dead drunk in the back seat. When someone piped up that "These things have a wheelbase exactly the same as a diesel locomotive," they couldn't resist. At the level crossing of the Great Northern Railroad, half a block outside the packinghouse door, just past the dark shadows of the loading bay and its drifts of tumbleweeds, they drove the car onto the tracks and took off the wheels. With a last, black bottle of Canadian Club between them, they idled all the way out of the country, deep into Washington, in the night. When they finally woke, with a start, out of their warm, steamy sleep, they were at Ellisford, twenty miles south of the line, smashed into the bumpers at the end of the dead line outside the sprawling tin roof of the Omak packinghouse. This was the far north of the U.S.— an abandoned area. A wasteland. Indian territory. But to us it was—and is—southern, and exotic. There under a greasewood and gravel American moon they all tumbled out for a piss under the stars, and the crickets sang. With that hot desert wind blowing over them, soft as the skin of a rattler or the frictionless wing feathers of a burrowing owl, they shunted the car

into reverse and idled all the way back into Canada, talking
away the night. Through the swamps and willowscrub of the
Indian lands stretching both ways from the border, with the
moonlight flooding the car like a bird's cool breath, they
talked about women, and booze, and fruit, and war.

When they returned to the level crossing by the Similkameen United Growers Packing Shed, they pulled the wheels
out of the trunk and bolted them back onto the car. It was
5:30. The sun was just rising among the firs on the eastern
ridge, high up, at five thousand feet. It was time to go home
and change the morning round of sprinklers, then go in for coffee and the beginning of another day. They drove Ramsay and
his new Buick home, and left him there until he woke up with
a headache. While he slept it off, they went around, doing each
other's sprinklers, and his too, and one by one drifted home.
The grass was cold. The light was the colour of lead. It was
heavy. You moved through it as if you were underwater at
freeze up, or right inside the substance of light.

The Front Line

OVER TIME, DRINK itself became the religion of the valley and in the mid-seventies the drop-out rate at the high school rose to almost 70 percent as we all fought to integrate—or comprehend—an urban education that was dragging us away. The valley was delivered to us as an evil from which we had to escape. A physical life was considered an appalling waste—of use only to the second rate. This was the old British Columbia and I was raised in it, right up to my throat. You will find it nowhere unless you go into the Interior, unless you step out of the twentieth century and into the earth. This is the front line of the battle. Here we are all cripples, to the last man and woman shelled by our own artillery, shelled by the enemy, harried by night raids; dark shapes slipping through the dark, and drugged with nightmare and drink and confusion, and speechlessness—words that do not connect with our world. The land is not something society wants within itself, and yet it is here. Society can only integrate it as an idea, but the earth insists on more. The old gods live.

Breathing

THAT YEAR IN Naramata when Hans Feldt lurched in bitterness out of the cherry tree to pass on to me, in the act of turning away, the future and the ownership of the land, we roasted
steaks in the coals to celebrate the end of cherry picking. I
drank a bottle of dry Portuguese wine the flavour of rust,
drank away a month, three hundred and sixty hard hours of
harvest, in which I tried to do the work of one tractor and
three or four men because I knew no other way to find worth
in myself. I had learned nothing else from my father. That
night I erased my whole life. I threw my whole life up. I sat
blankly in the cold grass with the stars towering overhead.
The black fronds of the trees swayed beneath the stars like
shadows of themselves, primeval—tall, sinuous birds.

That was the summer we would walk out into the lake as far
as we could, and then dive, hugging the cold sand at the bottom, rebreathing the air in our mouths and our lungs over and
over until we could go no farther. As the back pressure built
up within our skulls, we floated up to the surface like trout rising to snap a fly out of the bottom inches of the air. Then we
suddenly broke free, in the calm black water, two hundred feet
from shore, breathing, breathing deeply, and we were happy
with that.

Chrysanthemums

I SIT INSIDE tonight with a cut-glass vase of chrysanthemums the colour of dried blood. The whole room is filled with their thin scent. On the transparent waves of the air it is a music and replaces the air in my mind with itself. So it is there that the flowers bloom, and when I reach out my hand to touch them in the vase on my desk I am touching my past.

My mother had one of the largest flower beds in the valley. When I was five years old I would go around with her to the old ladies in the valley to collect plants, and then out again to plant them. There were fifty kinds of flowers there, from crocusses to carnations, daisies to lilacs, and, in the last dry-leaf hours of the fall, chrysanthemums, flowers the colour of dried flowers, of pippin apples, with the earth showing easily through the colours, flowers the colour of dreams, and of love.

It was among those flowers that I first saw the dancing, drifting scarlet of poppies. Their stems oozed with an opium-thick white glue—like Lepage's White Bondfast. It was bitter to the taste. No one told us it was poison.

In later years, when I was working on Brian and Tricia Mennell's frozen vineyard, above Similkameen Station, Mount St. Helens blew and the ash drifted down for days, giving a perpetual evening to the air. I then came to prefer dandelions over all other flowers—for their subtlety of colour and for their white seedheads, so full of light itself and of themselves only what could amplify the light. But now again, as I did when I was a child, I prefer the poppies and the mums. They are a distillation, a richness added to the air. They speak of generations of human care, flowers created on purpose for no other purpose than their own creation.

Capital

MY MOTHER WAS never a strong woman. As the years on the farm wore her down further and further she gave up more and more on the garden, until we finally tore it up, and the vegetables behind it, and put in lawn. That was the year my father came to understand the meaning of capital. We did not have to kill our own chickens any longer, or salt down grated cabbage in the basement, or brew our own beer. Nor did we have to bury carrots in a deep pit in the garden and, as the snow whipped gritty and sharp over our faces, our fingers numb and nearly useless from even one minute out in the snow, grub down into the warmth of the earth for their damp and their heat. That was the year the dreams began to erode with fatigue.

We hurled my mother's flower garden over the edge of the hill that spring, yet even to this day, after twenty years, the yellow irises thrive there. Cast out among the sage and cactus and rock-crocusses, and unirrigated, they have spread to cover sixty square feet, and bloom tall and rich, like a small sun on the slope, busily converting spring meltwater into light. I've seen no other irises with such colour. I think when we are young we long for the colours of the earth and later, just as I have done with farming and my mother did with those flowers, we throw them away. Against the pressures of society and income and against the pressures of the self, which they are meant to serve and nurture, they cannot hold up. And we miss these things intensely.

I still go from farm to farm checking on the work of my friends, spending a few hours with them, with my pruning clippers, and sharing gossip and thoughts and my life. And just as my mother did with flowers, I collect old apple varieties.

That are dying out.

The Colonial Dream

THE TRUE COLONIAL dream is that this land can be made into paradise, a whole society made out of an approach to earth and land. In this country called the Interior we import what we need of society—books, ideas, laughter—and export what we produce in contact with the soil, our foundation. We are a people without money, buried in work and the relentless, unforgiving obligations of time and history, which we call the land. It is all we have. We have oriented ourselves to the physical earth, and have left all other parts of social life to others, in England, or Toronto, or Germany—or L.A. The irony of the dream is that we speak for equal rights in a society which does not know of our existence, and if it ever heard of us would dismiss us as something of the past, some time of the past, something of no present life. The dream is to live so far back in the past that it is nearly impossible to surface for air.

It is to erase the self and replace it with that ancient conception of space, stars and trees swaying, moving, dancing in the night wind, silent like water.

Production and Worth

WITH A POSSESSED father trying to flee deep into the world, all I really had in the way of a childhood was the earth—wind streaming over my face and the scent of rain in dust; rain that for a moment returns dust to that first instant when it chipped off a rock-face in storm, the sharp scent of the earth, spinning in space, rain that gets in between the molecules of rock to shatter it yet farther, in re-creation of its original sundering; but I had nothing of human—commercial or political—worth.

I ran a thinning crew in Kelowna in 1976, and for six weeks the apples spat and hissed into the grass around us, like fire. In that summer of near-endless rain when I was eighteen years old I rode those workers hard. They must have hated me immensely. The boss would come down daily from his hand-built, glass-fronted house on the hill—built when the industry still had a sense of duration to it—and I would tell him that his workers were no good. Then I would ride them harder. I snapped at them about how to place their ladder in the tree, to use both of their hands, even when balancing on the top of the ladder on a steep hill. "If I can't hear that fruit falling constantly into the grass, then you're not working," I'd say, echoing Max Kohler to my father in 1953, at Chopaka, before the world. We must produce and not mind the pain: we don't count, the work counts, the work must be done, and always more, always past our limit, so that what is achieved is always

the limit. Life lived for a 1930's German vision of the state—
the surrender of the individual to time and fate.

When we took a break from thinning to weed a new planting
of apples, the sweat streamed down over us and as quickly
evaporated into the breezeless air. The unexpected sun beat
over and over at our foreheads like a mallet. Instead of cooling
us, our sweat only inflamed us further. Our mouths were as
dry as the burnt-up leaves of the thistles. When we put our lips
to the hydrant, the cold water felt hot on the hot skin of our
faces and chests. Only the pocket gophers were cool, burrowing beneath us with their small dark eyes and hooked feet, eating the roots of the trees like candy, in the dark. Pruning that
spring I had stepped through the sod, down into the soft, dried
grass of one of their nests. The new gophers were half the size
of my thumb—thin, helpless sacs of flesh, their eyes covered
with veils of skin. They quickly died in the cold. There in that
wide open sky I felt jinxed and hopeless. The world was
empty. The god was standing behind my back. If I turned
around he would strike me hard with the back of his hand and
I would hurtle to the ground. He was terrible, and huge, and
shadow. I was in charge, I said, and I would damn well say
when we went in or when we did not. "I don't feel any goddamn heat," I said.

When Tom came down to our work that morning the workers surged over to him right away. "Put the work off until
later," they pleaded. "Sure," he said. "We're all in this together. Work when you want to."

That was the first blow. The next came a few days later,
when we finished thinning and Tom sent the workers over to
the neighbour, Ken Day, who'd had a hard time that cold, wet
summer keeping any workers on the farm: they'd rather be in
Quebec, unemployed. The next day Ken told Tom he'd never
in his twenty years in the business seen anyone work so hard
thinning or move so fast or so well. When Tom told me, I was
shaken up for the rest of the summer.

That was the year my father sold his farm. In all the twenty-one years that he farmed in the Okanagan there was never a summer with so much rain and so little sun. The peaches rotted on the trees. The heavens were washing us away.

The Centre of the World

In 1953 MY father, a skinny young German with bad teeth, came to Max Kohler's cattle and fruit ranch at Chopaka for winter work. Going there was like going to Patagonia or up the Amazon. Chopaka is a jagged ridge rising right out of the riverbed half a minute over the Washington border. Against the sky she is a woman, naked, full-breasted, lying on her back, her head thrown back. The Salish of the Lower Okanagan, Indian Territory, called themselves the *O Kin O Kane*— those who live where they can see the top—of Chopaka. The Fujiyama of the West. The Holy Mountain. Ararat. The Centre of the World. Jerusalem. Delphi.

With Chopaka rising high across the river, and the river cutting the farm loose from it with a great, blue-silver ox-bow of light, and the mosquitoes flooding the shadows between in streams and swarms like squalls of crisp, dry rain, it is a beautiful and sacred site. Huge thunderstorms pour up out of the deserts of the Columbia and collect against the cupped thigh of that mountain with the hail streaming from the black clouds like solid light.

The orchard is planted on a fan of alluvial shale, on the higher ground to drain the frost; the cattle are kept in the sub-irrigated fields below; the bees range up through the alpine meadows and summer range—each brief flower like a small root fire bursting forth from the soil, giving us some hint of the earth burning below us. The bees feed on the sweet oozings of those flowers, and fertilize them. Out of heavy wax frames and the scent of pine and shavings, we collect their honey—white-suited, with screens over our faces, and each movement slow and measured—but they drink it from the flowers with their whole being, out of the dancing, burning soil.

The Unknown Country

WHEN MY FATHER arrived here, the connections between the Similkameen and the Okanagan, let alone the outside world of Vancouver, were slight. Today it is less of a world, and its people, true to themselves and their place, and their history of trapping, ranching, and Empire, are out of place—denied the very time in which they live. Time here is an old time. It once prevailed throughout British Columbia, but is now found only in silted mountain pockets. History here has had no break of modernism and nationalism—it is a continuous development and evolution out of Victorian times, and has not diverged from them.

The Wrong Valley

AFTER A WHOLE generation had fled to the cities in the fifties, farms here became nearly worthless. 1962 was the year my father bought his land, staking his claim to the future in the belief that, unlike the past and the present, it would not evaporate. Those were the last years of rural neglect, in the cycle that is descending on us again. Those were the years when the country had given up on colonization. Everyone was leaving the farm, abandoning the dream wholesale, because you cannot farm without a market, and you cannot sell the beauty of the land and the rituals of working the land, which are all you have.

"The place is like an oven," Dad would say. He'd take you by the arm, whoever you might be, and lead you out onto the veranda, supported by old steel water pipes buried in the ground and filled with concrete. Then he'd point west, through the feathery limbs of the elms, in the cool green light of evening. "You see that spur that comes down from the mountain, and that one on the other side? The valley is very narrow there. That's where it should be dammed. We could make a lake. Keremeos is up there. You know, we spent all night fighting the packinghouse fire, to save the town. When we were finished, and the town was saved, we stood around, wet, and dark, and said to each other, 'What in the hell for!' We had just realized what we had done!"

It was here my father bought his land, in the Similkameen, where society was a closed club and he was the invader, the outside world, the threat. That he worked so hard to break society up and remake it into a country was a result of his position here, not the cause of it. He thought this was Canada. He thought this, like Germany, was a country.

From the vantage point of time passed it's obvious he should never have entered a business whose products were sold through a co-operative system, where profit and loss were shared on a community level—a community he could not tolerate. Those colonial farmers were desperately trying to insulate themselves from the truth of their situation—that the world was trying to tear them apart, and had been trying to do so since the first of them fled here. My father was that outside world. When his efforts to rebuild the marketing system, and then his bitter efforts to tear it down, failed, it was the co-operative system that threw him out and banished him. That was the only effective power it had—to make true and visible what was always the case—like signing your name on a dotted line.

The Carrier

THE WAR OF my father's childhood was a war against all civilized people, and against history. By simply coming to the
Similkameen, however, he did not shake it off. In that time,
everything was forced into the physical; all terrors were made
real. It was a war of the dispossessed, against all who had
turned their backs on them, real or imagined—from the bank-
ers and landlords, to the middle-class, to the workers themselves. Over and over the returned soldiers of WWI heard they
weren't working hard enough, they had not fought hard
enough—those men who had been trained only to kill—or, better, to be killed—and who had nothing else to offer civilian, or
private, life. The Second War was their revenge and their solu-
tion: the war against everyone who had stayed at home, and
their children, and their world.

These wounds were what my father brought to this valley of
green evening night, where mosquitoes ride the wind for two
thousand feet above the river, streaming through the long
shafts of the late sun at such an angle they spill and flow like
smoke. When I grew up I hardly even noticed the wind but
bent to it like a sailor on ship or like a tree holding to its roots
on a bare ridge high above the river, but he felt it all the time,
burning in his face.

The entire old town of Keremeos torn down, board by
board, because to my father it was old junk from the past, because he didn't need a past, because all he needed was a future.

Late Talk in Stale Air

THE GERMANY I knew as a child was at my mother's feet in the stale, blue clouds of pipe-smoke that hung almost to the floor in my grandparents' house. There was only about a foot of clear air above the carpet, and my brother and sister and I instinctively tried to burrow down into that. Over the hours, as my father and grandfather grew louder and louder, I wanted to run outside into the wind, but I could not. In that dull, claustrophobic room, in which thought was without thought, full of pat answers and unheard questions, I learned, after a fashion, to think. The conversation was always one and the same: on my grandfather's part, socialism, on my father's, capitalism. Neither of them ever budged. Yet that stern, hard, stubborn and awkward man is the man my father loved above all others, the father he never had and has looked for always, in all things.

From my grandfather I have a few sentimental records: the Pastorale, the Fifth, where fate knocks on the door and Germany stands up out of the fog, *Eine Kleine Nachtmusik*, Confucius, a rosewood bowl he turned on his home-made, hand-riveted lathe, a lamp fashioned from a knotted red and white length of juniper stump which he pulled down from a cliff over Okanagan Lake and towed home behind his sailboat, the Vagabond. I have the scent of pipe tobacco loose in a tin, tar scraped out of the pipe with a rusty penknife held between scarred and knotted fingers, scent of iron and grease and shavings from his workshop, rotten stench of the Samoyed Husky lying under the table. And I have his blue eyes, looking out to sea, in his childhood, in a different land, in the fog.

The Sea

As a boy my grandfather wanted to cast off into the black hills of the sea and drift on the sediment of the stars with the great diesels hammering in his head, all around him the cold of steel, and cold seeping in from the sea. Those were the years before the war they said would, in its savagery and tactical stagnation, end all wars, the war that seemed impossible to win and consequently was not to be considered— the war that would never happen, because Germany looked out to the earth, and for the first time saw itself there, equal to Britain, with colonies and an extended economic power. But the Great War did come, and at fifteen my grandfather went into the Navy—a poor, second choice to the life of a wanderer on a tramp steamer in the South Atlantic.

When Germany renounced military activity, in fact all activity that could lead to power, and poured its earnings into the treasuries of the West, it lacked the capacity either to create an economy or to wage war, and the pressures to flee intensified. Forced from the sea, my grandfather became a machinist. Forced from work in the economic collapse of the twenties, he embraced socialism, the unity of Germany in the world. When the communists were driven from the streets by the National Socialists, he fled to Canada, and after the Second War he fled to the north, to escape the Bomb, and then, and again in retreat, to the Okanagan, broken by the land, to end his years building sailboats and sailing them on Okanagan Lake—at last.

The one time I sailed with him, it was a perfect day on the lake, without a ripple on the water or a cloud in the sky, only the sun filling the silent air, and the eyes able to drink it in, and the body able to fill with it, and dream, but children want to act on the world, and I was bored to the point of pain.

What I have of my grandfather is rage. "It was not the Americans who broke the back of the *Wehrmacht!*" I had never heard that word before. "It was the Russians!" This sudden passion for a long-renounced and long-dead country, astounded me. It was his gift—all he could pass on—a vision of errors repeated over and over again, and it was to be helpless against them, to see history so misrepresented one time more, when his whole life had been ruled and almost ruined by that history, and the convenient distortions of power.

1944

My FATHER DID not end his farming life in peace or fatigue, but in rage. The world is always collapsing to a thin point of white fire. This was the rage Hitler felt when he was overextended in Russia and suddenly knew that the War was lost, and knew it was his doing: this was the collapse of a dream no longer sustainable by the world, deflected into hatred for all parts of the earth that do not bend to the will; this was the love of straight lines: 1944, this was the world of my father when he was twelve years old—the eternal vision, the death of childhood, the cruel earth.

A Handmade World

MY GRANDFATHER made everything in his house, even the tools, the wrenches and screwdrivers, the hammers, anvils, chisels and home-made lathes he made them with. They were rough, ugly, cranky, greasy machines, in continuous disrepair, but they worked. Since he didn't know how to weld, all his machines, even his tractor, were riveted together. They shook apart as he used them, and he would rivet them back together again like an ancient smith throwing up sparks from his anvil. The anvil clanged in his workshop like a heavy bell. The air smelled like steel.

He packed a dozen shingle bolts, big, heavy blocks of red cedar dragged out of Stave Lake in the Depression, unsaleable even at a cent a piece, to Smithers, and then to Penticton, before he finally used them to shingle his chicken shed, in Cawston, in 1958. His children hated him. He threw nothing away.

Blind

My father's career in farming came to an end in five minutes of pain in the dust. He was farming in Benton City, Washington—trying to find in that southern country an image of freedom this country, and the fruit police, had failed to give. There in the desert just outside the iodine-poisoned bunchgrass of the Hanford Nuclear Reservation he used to line the Mexican wetbacks up under the sun. Since he needed a social security number he told them to give him ten numbers between one and ten. If they couldn't think of a number, he assumed they were too stupid to work for him. And there, while the Mexicans were out under the cherry trees with the forks and rakes they had made themselves out of branches to prove that it would cost nothing if Dad could let them work, the Cat would not start one morning, and the pressure burst: "Put the charger on it and go back in a couple of hours: it'll start! Do I have to do everything around here!"

After a couple of hours the Cat still wouldn't go. "You stupid ass!" he screamed, going purple in the face. He slammed the door against the wall, smashed down the steps, across the dusty yard, up onto the squat, yellow lizard-body of the Cat, grabbed the terminals of the charger and hooked them up to the battery. "There!" But in his haste he crossed the wires. The battery blew in his face and he went spiralling off into the dust—his face and eyes full of shrapnel and sulphuric acid.

The hired man tore off, spun the truck right into the ditch out-side the driveway, ran back for a second truck, and tore away, slamming from ditch to ditch. By the time the police picked him up five miles down the road he was walking—limping—and my father had been lying in the gravel for ten minutes, screaming.

The next day he was short one eye and half the sight in the other. He was no longer able to see. The work had him now, at last. History would no longer let him go.

The Storytellers

THIS IS THE way my father tells his stories: leaning forward, his whole body alive with a rough electricity. It is a beautiful art, of charm and smiles, an art of self-effacement, balanced neatly with aggression. The trick is to disappear, and then, once invisible, to consume the listener—so testing just how much of himself he can pour into his audience: the work of a master hypnotist.

Barracks-humour. Picked up in the bunkers along the Rhine in the late years of the War by a kid twelve years old.

A Parting of Ways

THAT BLIND SUMMER I was in the Similkameen, trying to return to my land, free of history. My brother had tried the year before—and had failed. Weakened by a terrible car-crash, his strength sapped by the socialism of the farmers and by the greasy workers from Quebec, he saw only weakness and fear and death. The god was there. He had finally made known his name: the god of death and vengeance. And there, during my first summer back in the valley, my parents tried to convince me to go to the States, but it was too important for me to come home, to the valley, not to the old farm—that was what I was praying the land would clear me of. When I travelled down there that summer to visit, we stepped into the farm office. It was two in the afternoon. For a minute Dad didn't recognize me. "Yes?" he said. "What do you want? Can I help you?"

Training the Young Spartans at Christmas, 1969

I HAVE THIS at least. In 1969 my parents spent Christmas in Germany. After thirteen years my father was finally taking his bride home to meet his family. By that time all the Germans who saw them off together in Penticton were no longer part of their lives. They were, themselves, finally on their own.

My brother and I were left to train the five acres of young Spartan apples. Enjoying our freedom, we got those two days of work done only half an hour before my parents came home. But my brother, already looking away from the land to his own form of freedom, didn't do a single tree. To beat the boredom he would pace around in the snow beneath the trees and insult my work—and yet he was unable to leave. And in a way, that was my childhood, my family, against the backdrop of a wild, impressionable land. This is where I learned the truth: where a man can see an opening, he takes it; there is no right. Here in Canada it was a child's—my father's—image of Hitler's cultural Darwinism that I lived, with his so-called restoration of the culture of the Nibelungs, who sacked Rome. Gangster culture. This is where you get with *Mein Kampf* and the frighteningly ordinary slogans of Auschwitz: "Freedom Through Work." If you say it, it will be believed. It is only words. It is there, a poison at the centre of the earth, to be guarded against, certainly not something you can erase just because you fight a war. The winning or losing comes later, the work of rebuilding on each side what war has destroyed and of shaping the terrors it has let loose. Death in war wins, always. He has a black face and a cold bitter breath.

Family, Farm

THE NIGHT OF my high-school graduation I left home. It was
2 a.m. I had my '57 Ford, which my brother had sold to me for
150 bucks: it had a hole in the gas tank, shot steering, a leaking
radiator, four colours of paint, and a bullet hole in the back
window. My hair was long and thick, over my shoulders,
frizzy, roughly brushed. My parents were bitter. I was bitter.
As I drove down the driveway, the grey rows of trees lit up in
the light of the car, the dust streaming behind me. Listening to
Leonard Cohen singing his songs of love and hate, I convinced
myself I had left everything behind, and through that act of
leaving I could enter my life—not forever leave it.

From that moment on, we were never a family again.

The farm was all we had.

As it was of no value to society, to Canada or to the world, it
fell apart under economic strain, and we all blew away with it,
not knowing for years that what we had lost was precious and
rare. The economics were nothing, only a way to try and fit the
farm, a living piece of the earth, into society, into the mind of
men, and it didn't work. The farm is an attempt to bring the
earth into society. It is wild and outside, as are the worlds we
live outside words. It was all a European dream and held together by the will alone until the dream vanished, dissipated,
could no longer hold out against the strain.

By turning his back on the other Germans in the valley my

father turned his back on his dream and eventually it dissolved and he lost himself, just as he had once turned his back on Germany and in that too lost his strength. He learned a new language while working on the orchards, but one with little depth. It wasn't the language of life but the language of fear and hate and failure, loneliness and exile, and inarticulateness, and loss. That is all he had, ultimately, to pass on, and with that I must fight and come clear. It is not the legacy or the land or the vision of life I would have chosen, but it is mine.

As I look back now on that time, more than anything else I have to say that it was there and then I was formed; and to all those who hurt me and to those I hurt in turn, as the madness ate into us, I say, let us remember it as it was. Love knows no morality. As soon as you judge, it is gone.

And it is this life I try over and over to remake as a life, over and over separating from it what is good and what in the passage of time, the passage into clarity, has already fallen away but which the usual, old familiar words and attitudes hide from us.

About the Author

Harold Rhenisch was born in Penticton, British Columbia, in 1958, and was raised on and by an orchard in the Similkameen Valley. After studying Creative Writing at the University of Victoria he returned to the Okanagan in 1981, dividing his time among his wife and two daughters, pruning and grafting fruit trees, and writing about his country, the B.C. interior. He has published four books of poetry with Sono Nis Press. Since the fall of 1992 he has lived in 100 Mile House, in the sky. Among his current projects arc a "revision" of Pound's *Cantos* and a sequel to *Out of the Interior*.